HAL LEONARD KEYBOARD STYLE SERIES

POST-BOP JAZZ PIANO

THE COMPLETE GUIDE WITH AUDIO!

To access audio visit:
www.halleonard.com/mylibrary

8655-1696-3731-1531

BY JOHN VALERIO

ISBN 978-0-634-06123-3

HAL•LEONARD®
CORPORATION

7777 W. BLUEMOUND RD. P.O. BOX 13819 MILWAUKEE, WI 53213

In Australia Contact:
Hal Leonard Australia Pty. Ltd.
4 Lentara Court
Cheltenham, Victoria, 3192 Australia
Email: ausadmin@halleonard.com

Visit Hal Leonard Online at **www.halleonard.com**

INTRODUCTION

What Is Post Bop Jazz?

Post bop jazz is not as easily defined as bebop or swing. There is no one particular post bop style, and there are no clear boundaries between post bop and pre-post bop jazz. Post bop is generally thought of as the style that followed bebop, but there are several styles that fit that description. Bebop flourished during the 1940s and 1950s and represents the beginning of modern jazz. Cool jazz and hard bop were outgrowths of bebop that flourished during the 1950s. Although they emphasized different aspects of bebop and refined the language in various ways, they are still contained under the bebop umbrella. Essentially, post bop is jazz that evolved after bebop during the 1960s. It may include remnants of bebop or even swing, or it may be far removed from any previous style of jazz.

Most jazz piano styles can be defined by the use of the left hand. Stride- and swing-era pianists preferred close position chords around the middle C area when choosing voicings. They usually alternated or mixed these chords with bass notes. The bebop pianists radically changed the left-hand function along with the right-hand approach. The almost-consistent quarter-note pulse of the left hand was replaced with random-like chordal jabs known as *comping*. The chord voicings were stripped down to two or three notes for the most part and were played lower than the middle-range swing voicings. Some pianists evolved from swing piano on a somewhat separate path from bebop; they used the same middle-register voicings as in swing, but eliminated the bass notes. They comped chords like the bebop players but played voicings like the swing players. In many ways, this path leads more directly to most post bop left-hand playing. Nat Cole, Milt Bunkner, Erroll Garner, Oscar Peterson, George Shearing, Red Garland, and Ahmad Jamal, among others, create a direct link to Bill Evans, who set the stage for modern jazz piano voicings.

How to Use This Book

The first part of this book describes the language of post bop piano playing. It includes chord voicings, scales, and modes, and their applications to harmonic, melodic, and rhythmic practice. Part 2 offers in-depth analyses of the five major post bop pianists: Bill Evans, Herbie Hancock, McCoy Tyner, Chick Corea, and Keith Jarrett. Each chapter closes with an original tune written in the style of the player examined.

The most valuable resources for learning any jazz style are the recordings themselves. The reader should read and practice all of the procedures and techniques described in the first part of the book. One should learn all voicings, scales, etc. in all possible keys. While reading the individual pianists' chapters, play through the examples and listen to some of the artists' actual recordings. Playing through the tunes at the end of these chapters should give the reader a feel for some aspects of each pianist's personal style. After playing and studying the tunes, the reader should refer to the lead sheet versions at the back of the book to freely interpret them as well as play along with the audio.

About the Audio

The accompanying audio features many of the examples in the book, performed either solo or with a full band. The tunes written in the styles of the featured pianists include accompaniment. These tracks can be used to practice comping and soloing in the post bop style. (To play along with the tracks without the piano part, turn down the right stereo channel.)

CONTENTS

Chapter 1
LEFT-HAND VOICINGS

The harmonic language of post bop piano is extremely rich and varied. It includes all the chords and voicings that preceded it, plus a seemingly infinite variety of newer harmonies and voicing concepts. Before studying harmonic innovations of the post bop pianists, the reader should be familiar with basic tonal theory and jazz harmonic practice.

Chord progressions form the background for most jazz improvisation. Understanding the relationships among chords is fundamental to voicing chords and improvising melodies. If you know the basic chord structures and relationships, you can comprehend and play music using formations that are more complex. Two basic aspects of harmony should be known before proceeding to complex formations: 1) basic seventh and sixth chords; and 2) basic chord functions within a *tonal* context (within the context of a key).

Once a chord is known or chosen, the pianist must choose an appropriate voicing. When dealing with close position chords, three factors come into play: 1) the particular voicing itself; 2) the registral placement of the voicing; and 3) the voice leading to and from the voicing. All of these components give each chord a particular sound. Tone color is a crucial element when choosing modern chord voicings. Often, voicings are selected for the way they sound more than for the harmonic information they impart. Post bop pianists use a wide range of chord extensions, alterations, and voicings to enrich their palette. To affect this rich palette of tone colors and harmony, pianists began to rely on a new concept known as *rootless voicings*.

Four-Note Rootless Voicings and Formulas

Rootless chord voicings evolved mostly during the 1950s. Ahmad Jamal, Red Garland, and a few others used them often, but **Bill Evans** was the first to systematize them and put them to consistent use. One can trace the origins of the post bop voicings also to include Nat Cole, Milt Bunkner, Erroll Garner, Oscar Peterson, and George Shearing. Essentially, rootless voicings are chord voicings without the root of the chord. Playing the root, then, is left to the bass player—who may or may not choose to do so. By eliminating the root, the pianist is free to play *chord extensions* beyond the 7th with just the left hand. These extensions typically include the 9th and 13th for dominant chords, and the 9th for most other chords. The standard tones used for basic rootless chord voicings are: 3–5–7–9 for major seventh, minor seventh, and minor/major seventh chords; 3–5–6–9 for major and minor sixth chords; and 3–13–7–9 for dominant seventh chords. (Diminished and half-diminished or m7♭5 chords will be discussed later in this chapter.) When using these voicings, seventh and sixth chords actually become ninth chords, or ninth chords with an added 13th.

Note that these are voicings for chords and not chords themselves. It may seem strange to call, for instance, the first chord a Cmaj7 when it is spelled and sounds like an Em7 chord! But keep in mind that a bass player will usually supply (or imply) the root, and the voicing will be heard clearly as a Cmaj7. Try practicing each voicing in the right hand while supplying the root in the left hand, as well as playing each voicing in the left hand alone.

Inversions

The tones in each of these voicings can be inverted, deriving the following voicings:

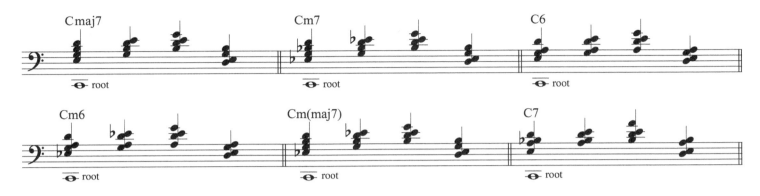

These voicings can be arranged into II–V–I formulas that progress through smooth voice leading. Below are the two most common formulas for major keys.

Rootless Voicing Formula 1 (RVF 1): Major Keys

Notice that only one note changes between the II and the V chords, and between the Imaj7 and the I6 chords. Each change is by step. Of course, V7 chords can progress to either Imaj7 or I6 chords, and not necessarily to both as above. This formula works the same in all major keys. A few examples follow.

Rootless Voicing Formula 2 (RVF 2): Major Keys

Notice that RVF2 uses the same notes as RVF1—but in a different order. The voice-leading principles are similar. As before, either a major 7th or 6th chord can be used as the I chord. Again, this formula works the same in all major keys. A few examples follow.

Some theorists refer to RVF1 and RVF2 as A and B forms, respectively. Notice that the bottom note of each voicing is the 3rd or 7th of a seventh chord, or the 3rd or 6th of a sixth chord.

Choosing Formulas

When choosing one form or formula over another, two factors come into play: pitch range and texture. Rootless voicings should not be played too low, or they can become "muddy"—also, the lowest note might be heard as a root. The lower and upper limits for left-hand rootless voicings are generally the C below middle C and the Bb above middle C. Of course, there are exceptions. RVF 2 contains minor 2nds in the II and V chord voicings that create "rubs" and thereby have more tension than the II and V chord voicings in RVF 1. Notice the different effect that each formula has on the same melodic line below.

Range considerations make some rootless positions more practical than others. For the keys of C, Db, D, and Eb, RVF 1 is used primarily. For the keys of Gb, G, Ab, and A, RFV 2 is used more often. For the other keys—Bb, B, E, and F—either formula works well. For variety and special effects, any position can be used in any key.

Altered Chord Tones

Notes of rootless voicings can be altered without altering the formulas themselves. Dominant chords are the most frequently altered chords. Examples of altered dominant chord voicings follow.

Examples of RVF 1 and RVF 2 using these altered dominants follow.

Added Chord Tones

Tones can be added to the basic rootless tones by either adding or substituting notes. The 6th or #11th is often added to a major seventh chord by adding it or substituting it for the 5th. Adding a 7th to a major sixth chord is the same as adding a 6th to a seventh chord. A #11th can be added to a major sixth chord. Examples for RVF 1 and RVF 2 voicings follow.

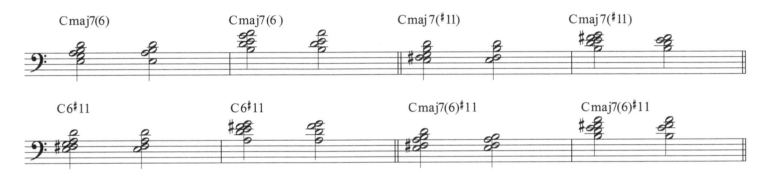

11ths and/or 13ths can be added to minor seventh chords in similar fashion.

Since the 9th and 13th are already part of the rootless dominant seventh chord voicing, the #11th can be added.

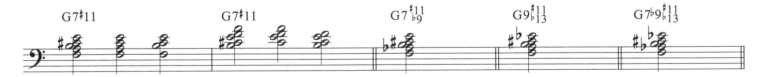

Examples of RVF 1 and RVF 2 using these added tones follow.

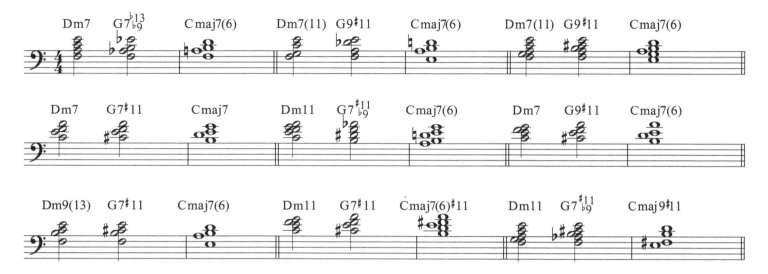

Suspended Chords

A common chord in post bop is the *dominant seventh suspended fourth* chord, usually notated as G7sus4, etc. There are two common ways of playing a rootless sus chord:

1. play a closed-position voicing in any inversion of the II chord that goes with the V7sus chord, such as Dm7 for a G7sus, or Gm7 for a C7sus, etc. (these chords are often notated as Dm7/G, Gm7/C, etc.)

2. play a rootless voicing in any inversion of the II chord that goes with the V7sus chord. For example, a G7sus rootless voicing would be the same as a Dm7 rootless voicing, and a C7sus rootless voicing would be the same as a Gm7 rootless voicing. (These chords are often notated as Fmaj7/G, B♭maj7/C, etc.)

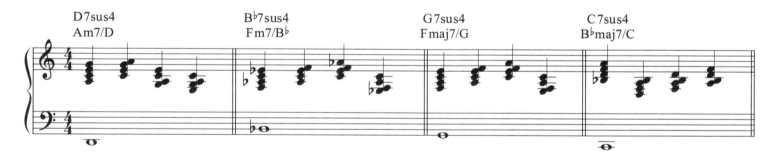

Below are examples of dominant sus chords coupled with II chords in a II–V progression.

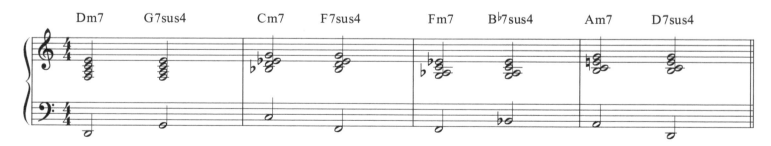

Diminished and Half-Diminished Seventh Chords

Diminished chords are usually ambiguous. Each chord traditionally has four possible resolutions. This is because the chord has a symmetrical structure consisting of all minor 3rds. When a diminished seventh chord is inverted, in turns into another diminished seventh chord whose root is a minor 3rd away. Therefore, there are really only three different diminished seventh chords:

1. $C°7 = E\flat°7 = G\flat°7 = A°7$

2. $D°7 = F°7 = A\flat°7 = B°7$

3. $E°7 = G°7 = B\flat°7 = D\flat°7$

Diminished and half-diminished seventh ($m7\flat5$) chords are voiced like major and minor seventh chords in the rootless system. The usual tones used are 3–5–7–9. But the 9th can be problematic. Since the $m7\flat5$ chord is usually associated with minor keys, the natural 9th can conflict with the third scale degree in the minor key where it usually occurs. Often, the best solution is to avoid the 9th altogether by playing the root instead.

Rootless Formulas in Minor Keys

The three $m7\flat5$ voicings shown above can be used in four typical ways in II–V–I formulas for minor keys. A I chord in minor can either a m(maj7), a m6, or a m7 chord. In the following examples only m(maj7) and m6 chords are used. The m7 chord can be substituted for these other minor chords, although technically a minor seventh chord is more properly a II, III, or VI chord in major keys than a I chord in minor keys. The natural 13th on the V chord can cause the same conflict as the natural 9th on the II chord, and both should be used with care. When there is no conflict the natural 9th and 13th are usually preferable. Four typical ways of playing RVFI and RVF2 in minor follow.

Rootless Voicing Formula 1 (RVF 1): Minor Keys

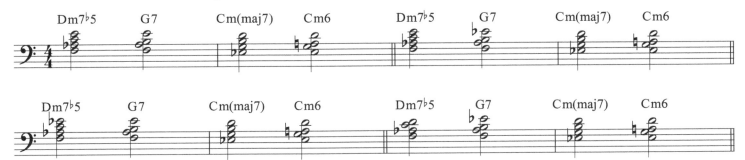

Rootless Voicing Formula 2 (RVF 2): Minor Keys

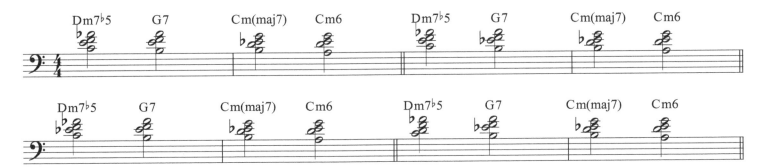

Added Tones

The 6th and major 7th can be used together in minor I chords, and the 11th is often added to m7♭5 (half-diminished seventh) chords.

Mixing Major and Minor Modes

Chords from the major and minor formulas often are mixed within a chord progression. Here are a few examples using RVF 1 and RVF2.

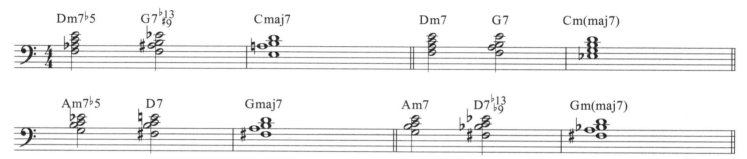

Other Rootless Voicing Formulas

So far, only two of the four possible positions for rootless voicings have been used. Although the other two, RVF3 and RVF4, are used less often, they are useful and offer the pianist more variety in choosing sounds for chord voicings. These are sometimes referred to as the C and D forms.

Rootless Voicing Formula 3 (RVF 3)

Rootless Voicing Formula 4 (RVF 4)

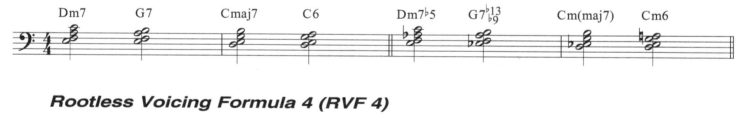

Altered and Added Chord Tones

All of the alterations and added notes used for RVF 1 and RVF 2 can be used for the new formulas as well. A few samples follow.

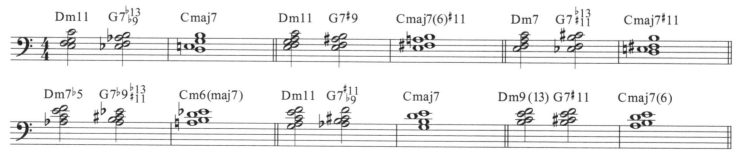

Three-Note Rootless Voicings and Formulas

The most common three-note rootless voicings are derived from the four-note formulas. Here are three-note versions of RVF 1 and RVF 2.

Dominant chords can be altered as in four-note voicings.

Three-note minor-key versions of RVF1 follow. The same concerns for the four-note versions apply here as well.

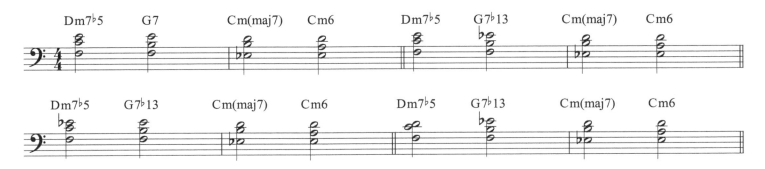

The flat 5th is an essential note in defining the m7♭5 chord, so the voicings used above are more ambiguous than their minor seventh counterparts (because the ♭5th is missing). Here are alternate versions of the three-note m7♭5 voicings that use the ♭5th instead of the 7th, coupled with dominant chord voicings only.

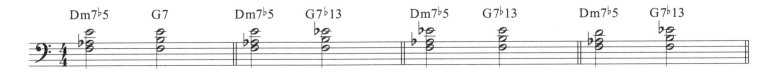

Three-note minor versions of RVF2 are simpler, because the 9th of the II chord (m7♭5) is not part of the voicing. That leaves only one possibility.

Dominant Seventh Voicings and Tritone Substitutions

Tritone substitution relates to the interchangeability of dominant seventh chords whose roots are a tritone apart. A D♭7 can substitute for a G7; an E7 can substitute for a B♭7; etc. The 3rd and 7th of one chord invert to the 7th and 3rd of the other chord. The 3rd and 7th of any dominant seventh chord form the interval of a tritone. The B–F tritone of a G7 chord, for example, inverts to the C♭–F of a D♭7 chord.

This makes for a lot of flexibility in dealing with scales, melodies, and bass lines. The bass player may be thinking G7, the pianist may be thinking D♭7♯9, while the saxophone player can think of either one, or some scale that relates to both.

Dominant chords are often cycled by maintaining a consistent voicing. The roots become ambiguous without bass notes. There can be several interpretations of these voicings.

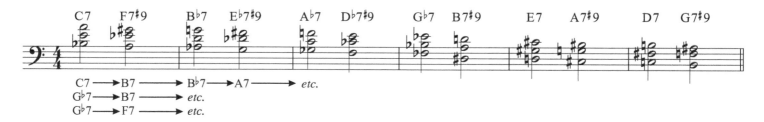

C7 ⟶ B7 ⟶ B♭7 ⟶ A7 ⟶ *etc.*
G♭7 ⟶ B7 ⟶ *etc.*
G♭7 ⟶ F7 ⟶ *etc.*

Two-Note Rootless Voicings

Rootless voicings can be reduced to just two notes. Bill Evans and others used two-note voicings for thinner textures and guide-tone harmonizations. The rule is simple: play only the 3rd and 7th (or 6th) of a chord.

Formulas based on RVF 1 and RVF 2 are shown here.

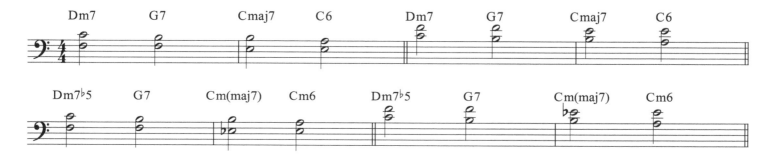

Two-note voicings are often used for dominant seventh cycles. Notice that you can adjust each tritone voicing enharmonically to form the tritone of the dominant seventh chord that lies a tritone away.

Cluster Fragments

Cluster fragments are usually two- or three-note voicings that do not contain all essential chord tones, namely 3rds and 7ths. They usually contain a 2nd (most often a minor 2nd) between the two lowest notes. Bill Evans and others have often played fragments in place of the more standard rootless voicings. Fragments often contain the root, but lack either the 3rd or 7th. Below are typical fragments used for some basic chord qualities for the root C.

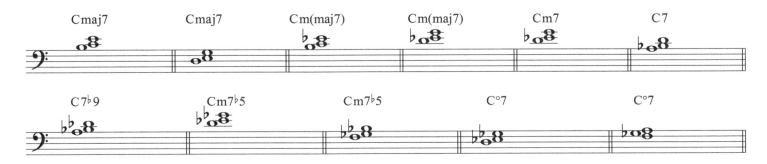

One fragment voicing can be used for several different chords. This one consists of a minor 2nd and major 3rd.

This fragment consists of a minor 2nd and minor 3rd.

Clusters made entirely of 2nds are also possible.

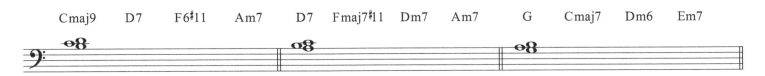

Fragments in Formula Voicings

Cluster fragments can be used in place of four- or three-note voicings in otherwise rootless voicing formulas. A few examples follow.

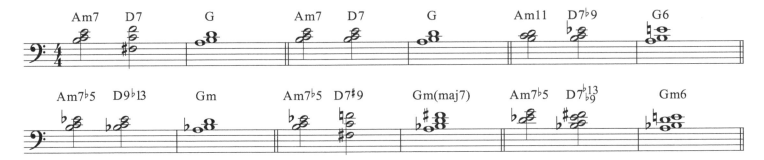

Quartal Voicings

Quartal voicings are those built entirely on 4ths. For the left hand, that usually involves three notes. During the 1960s, quartal voicings became very popular with many post bop pianists, including McCoy Tyner and Chick Corea. Bill Evans was the first pianist to work out quartal voicings for two hands. His contribution to the Miles Davis album *Kind of Blue* sparked the interest in voicing chords primarily in 4ths instead of 3rds. Open 4ths have an open sound that is ambiguous out of the context of a chord progression, and quartal voicings tend to blur tonal implication and direction. This suited the non-traditional tonal contexts of much 1960s jazz.

Below are some common left-hand quartal voicings. All of them contain at least two notes from the basic seventh chord that they represent.

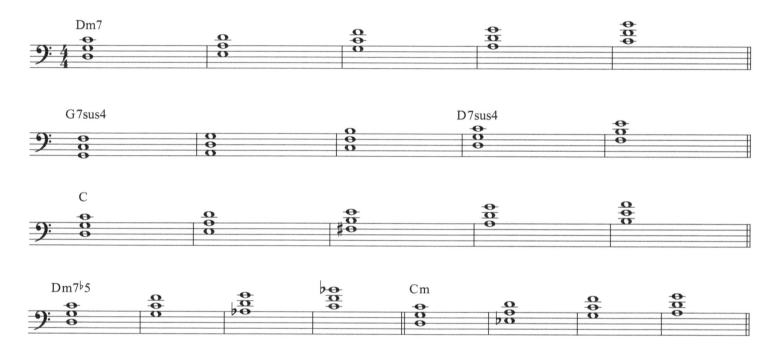

Quartal voicings are often used together to create consistent textures. Here are some ways they can be used in II–V–I progressions.

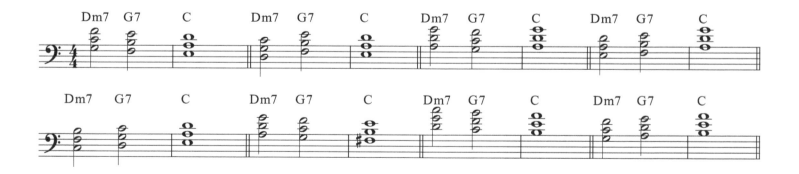

Combined Voicings

The voicings and voicing formulas described so far refer to general principles and formulaic procedures used by post bop pianists. In actual practice, however, voicings and voicing formulas are often mixed; no one particular texture or voice-leading formula holds sway. Five-, four-, three-, and two-note voicings can be mixed within a harmonic phrase, and smooth voice leading can be interrupted to create tension, textural and timbral variety, and melodic interest within the chord progression.

Inverted Major Seventh Chords

Inverted major seventh chords are often used within a mostly rootless voicing context. The rub of the major 7th against the root fits in well within the sonic realm of rootless voicings. The minor 2nd produced in these inversions gives a sound akin to some rootless positions of other chord qualities. Thus, although not technically a rootless voicing, the inverted major seventh chord can be seen as a part of an otherwise rootless system. Here are some samples of combined rootless voicings and inverted major seventh chords in typical progressions.

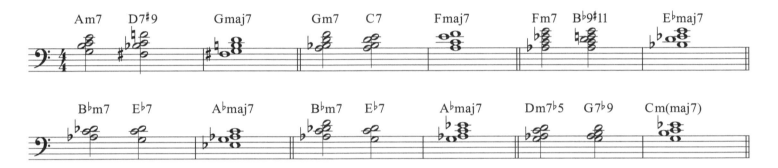

Other voicings with roots can be mixed with rootless voicings, and any combination of root and rootless voicings can be used. Examples in the styles of Bill Evans, Herbie Hancock, and Keith Jarrett follow.

15

Left-Hand Comping

Comping refers to the chordal accompaniment of a melody. The pianist typically comps with two hands while other instruments play melodies or solos. When the pianist plays a melody or solo, he or she will usually play it in the right hand while comping with the left hand.

There are essentially two different ways to approach left-hand comping; the first is with a consistent rhythm, and the second is with a random-like rhythm. A consistent rhythm might be a groove-like formula as shown below.

Ahmad Jamal and Red Garland made much use of the pattern shown below. The chords anticipate beats 1 and 3. An example in Jamal's style follows.

The reverse of the rhythm shown above is used less often but is also common. Here, the chords anticipate beats 2 and 4. An example in the style of Bill Evans follows.

Playing a regular pattern in the left hand relates more directly to the pulse than to the right-hand rhythms. It sets up a rhythmic anticipation that establishes a groove and creates rhythmic reference points for the right-hand melodies.

Random-like comping is more typical than consistent comping. Here the focus is more on the right-hand rhythms. The comping rhythms relate more to the right-hand rhythms than to the pulse. Durations of chords are an important part of comping. Below is a left-hand example in the style of Bill Evans. Notice the rhythmic and durational variety.

Chapter 2

VOICINGS FOR TWO HANDS

Root-Position Open Voicings

Open voicings for two hands can be categorized according to their interval structure. Below are examples for a Cmaj7 and a C6 chord. Note that a major sixth chord can substitute for a major seventh chord without affecting the voicing category or function. There are five basic types considered here, starting with A-type: 1–7–3–5; B-type: 1–3 (10)–7–9; C-type: 1–3 (10)–5–7; D-type: 1–5–3–7; and E-type: 1–5–7–3. These voicings apply to all other chord qualities.

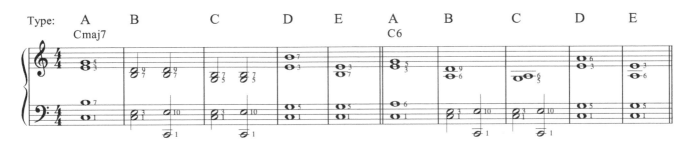

Open Voicing Formulas

As with rootless voicings, these voicings often combine into convenient voicing formulas. Here are some typical II–V–I formulas in major keys. Types A and B alternate easily when the root of each successive chord moves down by a 5th. Note that a 1–3 left-hand voicing can replace the 1–10 voicing in any of these examples.

The same voicing formulas apply to minor keys.

Extended and Altered Chords

These voicings can be adapted to include extended and altered chord tones by adjusting one note. Here are some common examples.

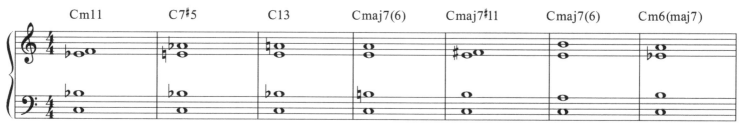

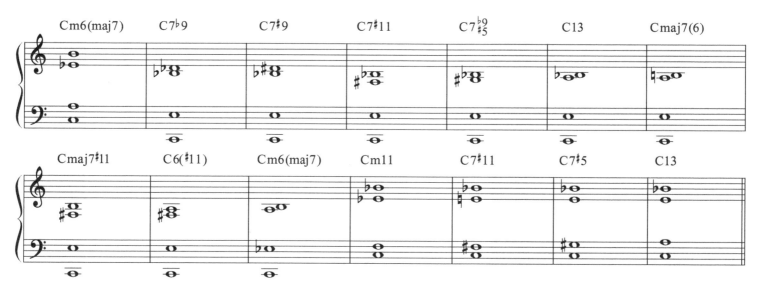

Notes can be added to the basic open voicings to create extended five- or six-note chords. Some minor seventh chord voicings follow.

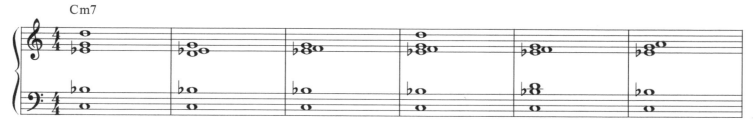

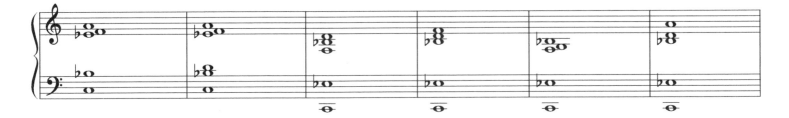

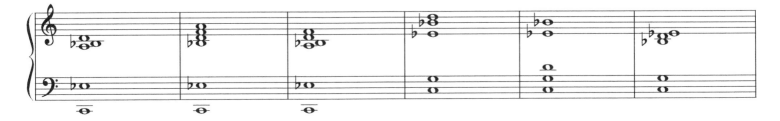

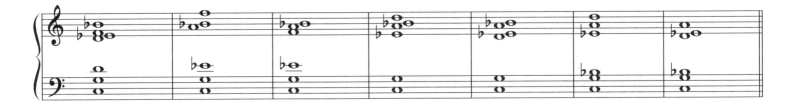

Here are some extended dominant seventh chord voicings.

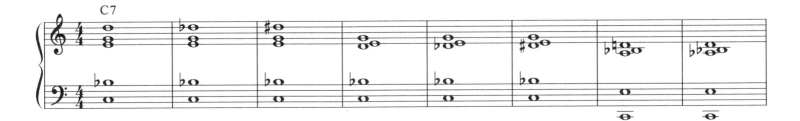

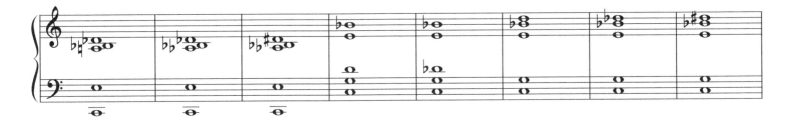

Some major seventh and sixth chord voicings follow.

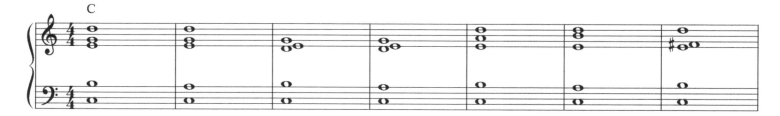

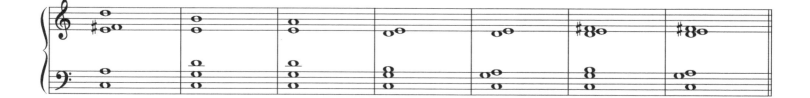

All other chord qualities can be voiced in similar ways. Doubling, displaced notes, and variations in spacing add variety and timbral nuances to all of these voicings.

Polychords / Upper Structures

A chord voicing can take on the appearance of one chord superimposed on another chord. The term *polychord* usually refers to a voicing of a chord rather than two simultaneous chords. The same technique is often referred to as *upper structure* (the upper structure being the upper chord). The upper chord is usually a triad, but a seventh chord is possible. Polychords are usually used for dominant chords, but can be used for other chord qualities. The most common dominant polychords are shown here.

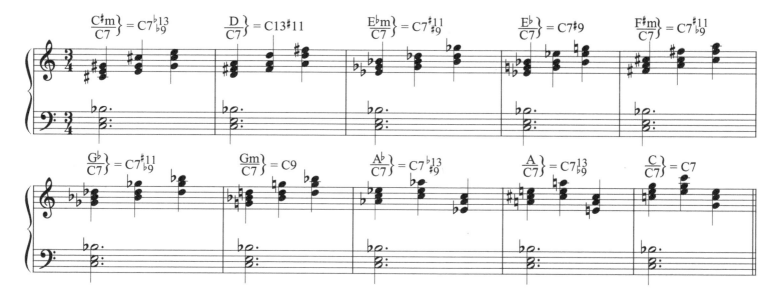

Notice the tensions that each polychord produces and the different effects of each inversion of the upper structure. Also, the C major triad is included here as an upper structure. Although a C major triad is implicit in a C7 chord, voicing it as an upper structure yields some interesting sounds that reinforce the natural overtones of the root.

Four-note upper structure triads that span an octave played over rootless dominant voicings are used often in comping. Herbie Hancock made this approach popular during the 1960s (See Chapter 6). A few examples follow.

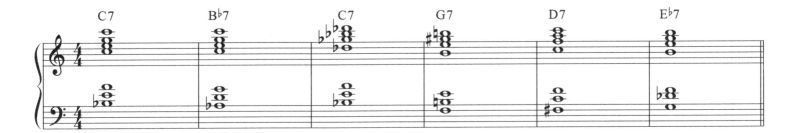

Examples of polychord possibilities and four-note triad upper structure for other chord qualities follow.

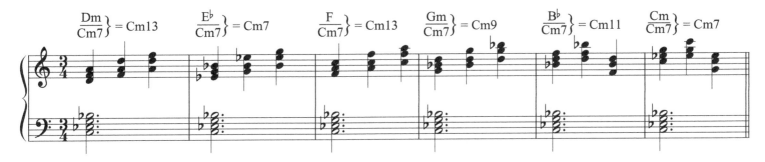

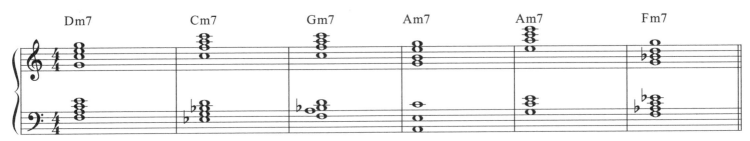

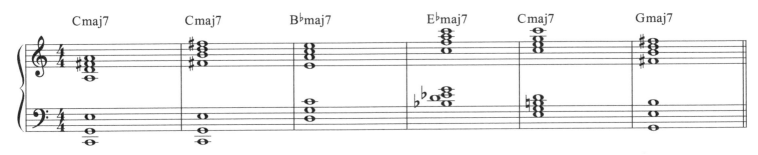

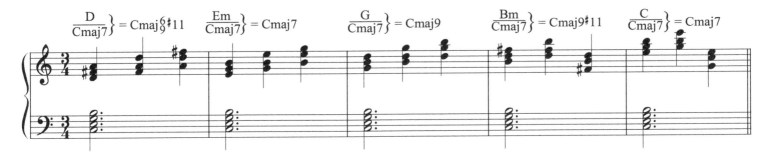

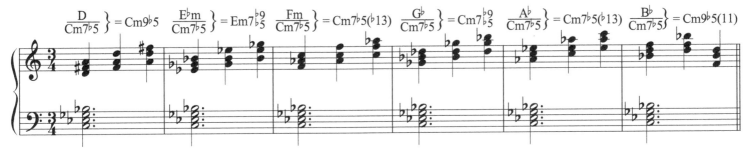

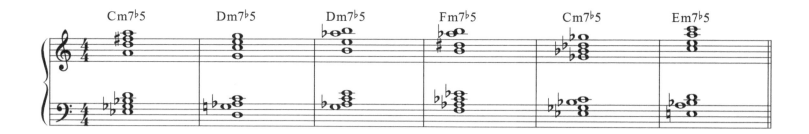

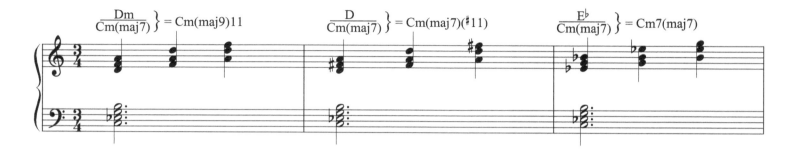

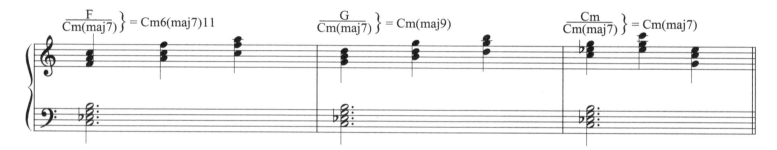

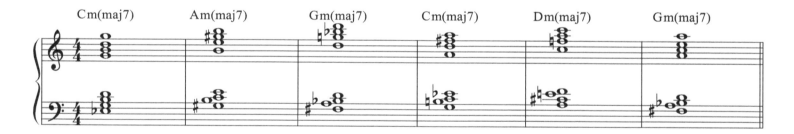

Upper Structure Arpeggios

Upper structure arpeggios are commonly played over a basic chord voicing. They can be used as decorative fills or part of an improvised line.

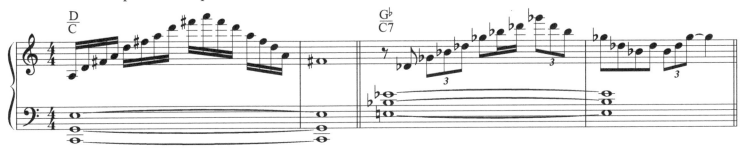

Open Rootless Voicings

Rootless voicings can be played with two hands, and they can be extracted from the left-hand voicings shown in Chapter 1. They are commonly used for comping. Each of the rootless voicing formulas can generate an open voicing formula for two hands.

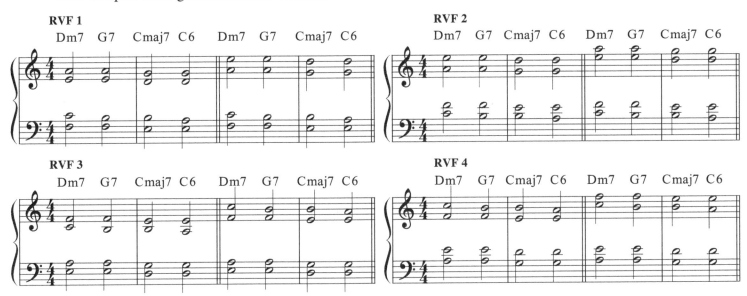

Quartal Voicings

During the early 1960s, voicings based on 4ths rather than 3rds became popular with certain pianists, most notably McCoy Tyner and Chick Corea. Although open 4ths sometimes occur in the rootless voicings described thus far, some pianists derived other quartal voicings and used them almost exclusively at times. Quartal voicings for two hands can be derived from the left-hand voicings described in Chapter 1. Common four-note voicings for each chord quality are listed here.

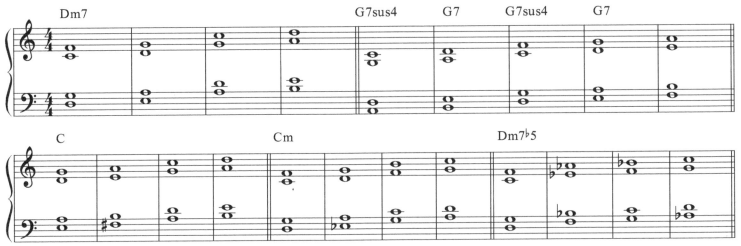

Five-note quartal voicings are also possible. Here are some common voicings.

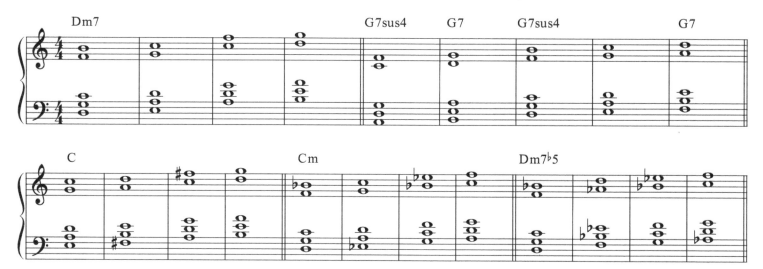

Another 4th can be added to the above voicings to create six-note voicings.

Tertial-Quartal Hybrid Voicings

"So What" Voicings

Bill Evans actually used a quartal-tertial hybrid voicing (constructed from mostly 4ths) on the Miles Davis tune "So What" (from the 1959 album *Kind of Blue*). These particular voicings have been referred to as "So What" voicings ever since.

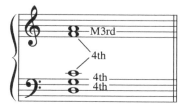

This voicing works for a Dm7, a B♭maj7, or an E♭maj7♯11 chord.

Combined Quartal and Rootless Voicings

Post bop pianists often combine rootless left-hand voicings with quartal right-hand voicings. These hybrid voicings are often used for comping. Some examples for II–V–I formulas follow.

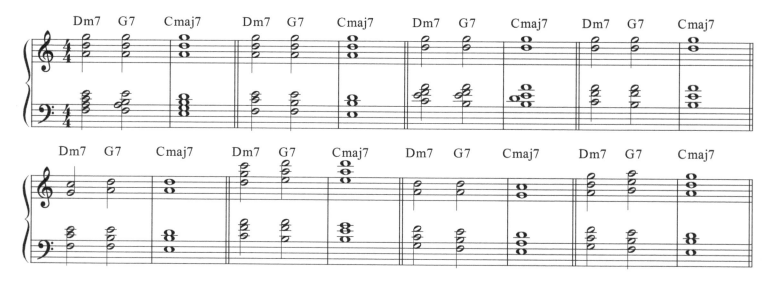

Combined Tertial and Quartal Voicings

Other tertial/quartal voicings are widely used for comping. Here are some possibilities.

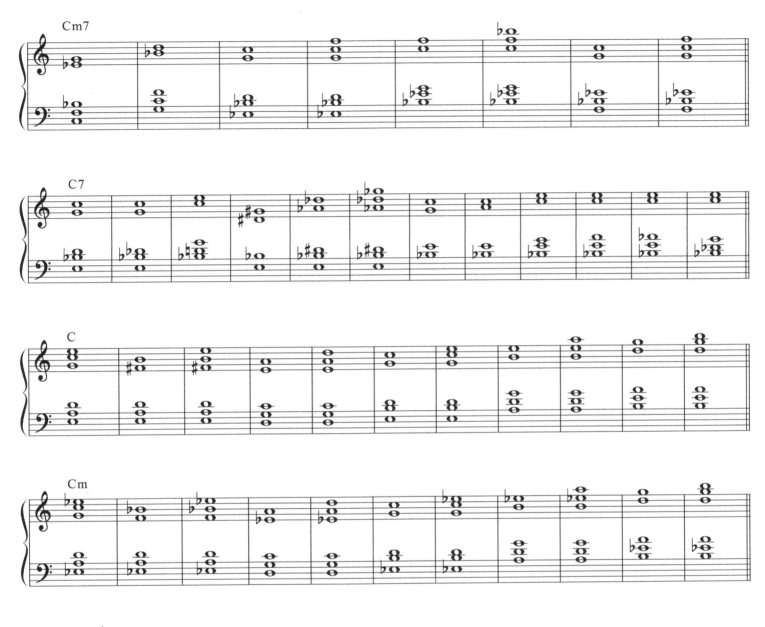

Locked Hands / Block Chords

During the 1940s and 50s several pianists developed a way of playing chord melodies with both hands, known as *locked hands* and/or *block chords*. Two characteristics of this approach influenced the post bop players: 1) the separation of the left hand from the pulse; and 2) the use of the left-hand voicing to "color" the melody notes.

Locked Hands

In its basic form, the locked-hands technique requires the right hand to play a closed-position voicing below the melody note, while the left hand doubles the melody note an octave lower. The pianist must decide how to harmonize each melody note; several options are available. Each melody note can be harmonized with: 1) notes from the prevailing harmony; 2) notes from the prevailing harmony on most chord tones, and passing chords inserted on non-chord tones; or 3) notes from the prevailing harmony on chord tones, and diminished seventh chords on non-chord tones. Each is demonstrated below.

Drop Two

A common variation on this technique is known as the *drop two*. The voicing is derived by dropping the second highest voice down one octave. This is accomplished in one of two ways: 1) keeping the right-hand voicing as is, and doubling the second highest voice an octave lower with the left hand, thereby producing a five-note voicing; or 2) dropping that note from the right hand, and playing the note one octave lower in the left hand.

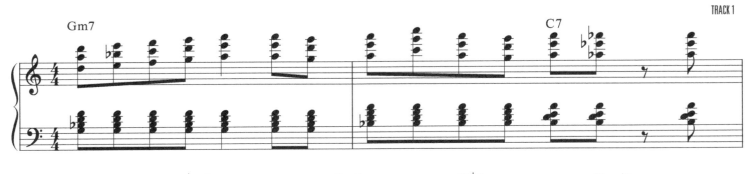

Block Chords

Pianists often play block chords in ways other than with "locked hands." Red Garland often played in a full two-handed style that featured middle-register chords in the left hand, and "ringing" octaves and 5ths in the upper register with the right hand.

TRACK 1

Chapter 3

SCALES AND TONALITY

Scale theories are somewhat new to jazz. *Scale* in this context refers to a collection of notes that serves as source material for a relationship among certain notes, rather than a stepwise melodic motion. Although the original bebop players were the first in jazz to base their improvised melodies more on scales than chords, they did not consciously do so.

Much has been written on the use of scales in modern jazz theory. This chapter will present the most important scales and their uses. Scales are used as source material for improvisation. Post bop players used many, more "exotic," scales along with traditional diatonic scales. In modern jazz theory, scales are derived from chords. A chord may suggest one or several scales to improvise from. Certain scales are considered to better express the quality of the chord, while others create more tension in relation to the chord.

Traditional Diatonic Scales

Major Scales and Modes

Traditional diatonic scales include the major scale, its derivative modes, and the various forms of the minor scale. The derivative modes of the major scale are obtained by starting a new scale with a new tonic on each successive scale degree; thus the D Dorian mode contains the same notes as a C major scale but starts on D. These modes are often thought of as corresponding to each diatonic seventh chord of the major scale. While some theorists think of the notes of a C major scale when played over a Dm7 chord as a D Dorian mode, implying D as a temporary tonic, the reality is that in this situation, C is still the tonic, and thus a C major scale is still operating. However, when scales that are foreign to the prevailing chord are used, the separate scale-per-chord approach is more useful.

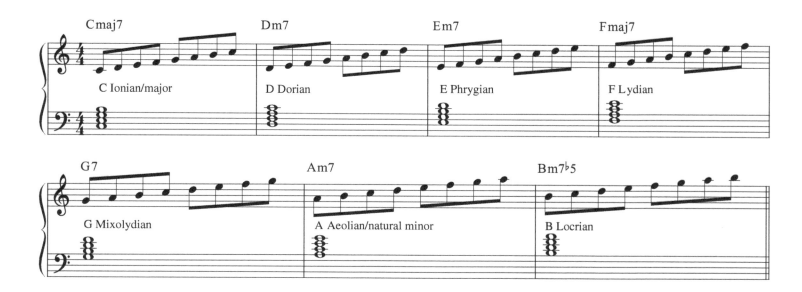

Minor Scales

Minor keys do not fit so neatly into scale theories. One reason is that there are essentially three different minor scales in traditional tonal music—natural (pure) minor, harmonic minor, and melodic minor. A fourth minor scale, known as *jazz minor*, is sometimes referred to—it is the same as the ascending melodic minor scale without changing for a descending version. Since the ascending melodic minor scale has a special significance in jazz theory, it will be referred to simply as the melodic minor scale.

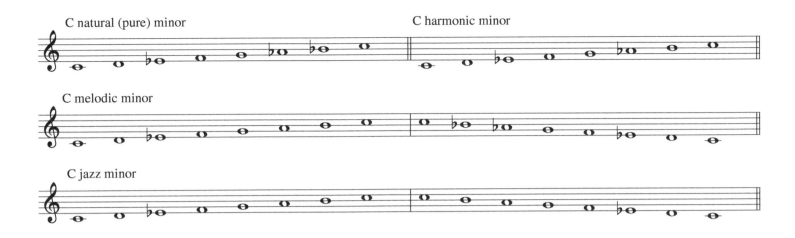

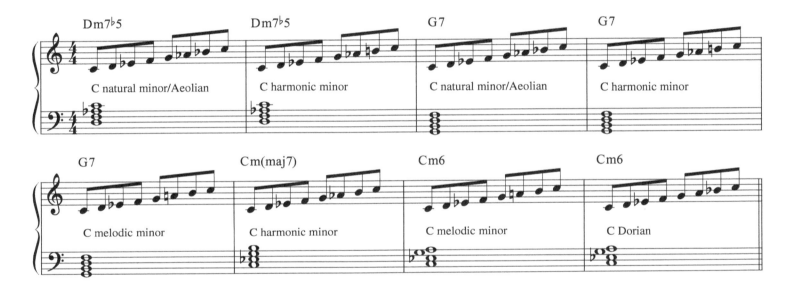

Since there are several scales used in minor keys, deriving diatonic modes or scales for each scale degree can be problematic. Scale choice depends on chord choices, which often depend on melodic considerations. A simple II–V–I progression in minor can imply the following scale choices:

Modes of the Melodic Minor Scale

Scales can be derived from the melodic minor scale in the same way that the traditional modes can be derived from the major scale. None of them, however, function as independent tonalities in the way that the traditional modes do. For instance, you can superimpose a Dorian mode on a II chord in major, but a Dorian mode also can exist as its own tonality. Music can be in Dorian as much as it can be in major. The so-called "modes" of the melodic minor scale are used over certain chords to add colors that are not available from traditional scales, but do not usually constitute tonalities in their own right. The following modes (scales) are derived from a C melodic minor scale.

29

The *Lydian dominant* and *Altered* scales are used extensively in post bop. There are many progressions in jazz that use a dominant seventh chord as a IV chord (F7 in the key of C major). The Lydian dominant scale works well in this situation, as the lowered 7th of the IV chord is accommodated by the lowered 7th degree of the F Lydian mode that is also the minor 3rd degree of the C minor scale. The scale also works well with any dominant ♯11 chord.

The *Altered scale* works with any altered dominant chord. It includes ♭9, ♯9, ♭5 or ♯11, and ♯5 (or ♭13). It's easy to think of an altered scale as containing the same notes as the melodic minor scale starting a half-step higher than the root of the chord. For instance: a C altered scale contains the same notes as C♯ melodic minor; an E altered scale contains the same notes as F melodic minor; etc. The altered scale is often used with altered dominant chords or to create tension on dominant chords in otherwise diatonic situations.

The *Locrian ♯2* scale is typically used with m7♭5 chords and is so named to distinguish it from the pure Locrian, whose second degree is only a half step above the tonic note. It works well when the major 9th is used in the voicing of the m7♭5 chord.

The *Lydian augmented* scale is used on maj7♯5 chords. Although relatively rare, this scale is sometimes used to spice up major seventh chords or to create unusual sounds.

The other modes from the melodic minor scale are less common and are referred to in the chord-scale chart later in this chapter.

The Diminished Scale

The *diminished scale* is an artificial, symmetrical eight-note scale consisting of alternating whole and half steps. The scale has two forms: the *whole-half* version and the *half-whole* version. The whole-half diminished scale is typically used with a diminished chord; the half-whole diminished scale is typically used with a dominant chord. For clarity of function, these scales will be referred to as *diminished diminished* and *dominant diminished*, respectively.

The two forms of the scale are symmetrical, as are diminished seventh chords; just as there are really only three different diminished chords, there are three different diminished scales that can be arranged in groups: C–Eb–Gb–A; C♯–E–G–B♭; and D–F–A♭–B. Each group contains enharmonically the same notes in different orders.

The Whole Tone Scale

The *whole tone scale* is an artificial six-note symmetrical scale made up of all whole steps. Essentially, there are only two whole tone scales; each uses half of all twelve available notes. When used in isolation, a whole tone scale is really tonic-less, thus there is no hierarchy of pitch relationships. The French composer Claude Debussy made extensive use of this to create a sense of floating or ambiguous tonality. Jazz players typically superimpose a whole tone scale on a 7♭5 or ♯5 chord; the tonality is implied by the dominant functioning chord.

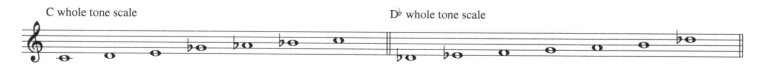

The Blues Scale

The *blues scale* was a staple of jazz from its beginnings, and its use continued in post bop. While the blues scale is sometimes isolated for stretches of time in improvised solos, players often play from a hybrid *blues/Mixolydian* scale.

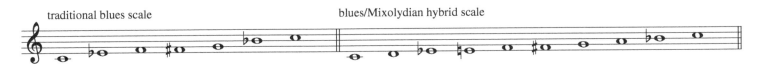

Pentatonic Scales

Two types of *pentatonic* (five-note) scales are commonly used in post bop: *major pentatonic* and *minor pentatonic*. They can be derived by extracting notes from the major and natural minor scales as shown below.

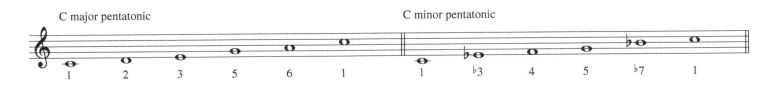

In post bop jazz, pentatonic scales are used primarily as superimposed scales, played over a prevailing tonality or chord. By restricting a melodic passage to only five notes, certain colors or chord tones can be emphasized. For instance, on a C major type chord, three different pentatonic scales are commonly played—C, G, and D major pentatonic. Each emphasizes different colors or chord tones.

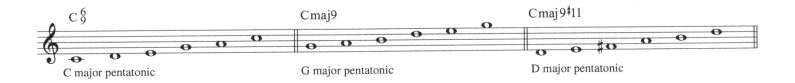

Pentatonic scales can be superimposed on other chord qualities as well. Below are common pentatonic scales for minor seventh and dominant seventh chords.

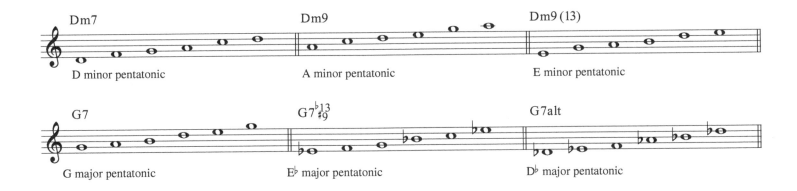

Scales and Improvisation

One can improvise with all these scales and others by associating certain scales with certain chords in certain contexts. For instance, a minor seventh chord can be a II, III, or IV chord in major keys or a I or IV chord in minor keys. Different scales should be applied accordingly. Below is a chart that can act as a guide. The list is not meant to be comprehensive, but to show some obvious possibilities. Bear in mind that scales are not a necessary component of improvisation; some players rely on them more than others do.

Chord Type	Function	Scales
maj7, maj6, maj9	I or IV in major III or VI in minor	major, Lydian major pentatonic from R, 5th, and 2nd blues from 6th
maj7♭5, maj7#11	I or IV in major III or VI in minor	Lydian
maj7#5	ambiguous	Lydian Augmented
m7	II in major	Dorian or major of prevailing key minor pentatonic from R, 5th, and 2nd diminished diminished (whole-half) blues
m7	VI in major	Aeolian or major of prevailing key minor pentatonic from R, 5th, and 4th blues
m7	III in major	Phrygian or major of prevailing key minor pentatonic from R, 5th, and 4th blues
m7	I in minor	Aeolian (natural minor) Dorian minor pentatonic from R, 5th, and 2nd blues
m7	IV in minor	Dorian minor pentatonic from R, 5th, and 2nd blues
dom 7 (unaltered)	V in major	Mixolydian or major of prevailing key Lydian Dominant major pentatonic
dom 7 (unaltered)	V in minor	Mixolydian ♭6 or melodic minor from 4th
7♭5 or 7#11	V in major	major pentatonic Lydian Dominant
7♭5 or 7#11	V in minor	whole tone
7♭9	V in major	dominant diminished (half-whole) Altered

Chord Type	Function	Scales
7♭9	V in minor	Altered harmonic minor of prevailing key
7♯9	V in major	Altered dominant diminished (half-whole) Dorian minor pentatonic blues
7♯9	V in minor	Altered Aeolian minor pentatonic blues
dom7 alt	V in major	Altered dominant diminished (half-whole) major pentatonic from ♭5th and ♭6th
dom 7	IV in major	Lydian Dominant
7sus4	V in major	Mixolydian or major of prevailing key minor pentatonic from 2nd and 5th
m(maj7)	I in minor	melodic minor
m6	I in minor	melodic minor Dorian minor pentatonic from root, 5th, and 2nd blues
m6	IV in minor	Dorian minor pentatonic from root, 5th, and 2nd
m7♭5	II in minor	Locrian harmonic minor of prevailing key
m7♭5(9) or m9♭5	II in minor	Locrian ♯2 diminished diminished (whole-half)
m7♭5	II in major	Locrian ♯2 diminished diminished (whole-half)
m7♭5	VII in major	Locrian
°7	VII in major or minor, V chord sub, or passing chord	diminished diminished (whole-half) harmonic minor of prevailing minor key

Chapter 4

MODALITY

Modal music differs from tonal music in that it is based on scales rather than chords. Chords may be used, but they do not direct the flow of the music. In modal music, the center of gravity is the tonic note; in tonal music, the center of gravity is the tonic (I) chord. Although modal music predates tonal music, it was not introduced into jazz until the late 1950s. The first major attempt at using modes in jazz, Miles Davis' *Kind of Blue*, paved the way not only for modal jazz, but post bop as well.

Tonal music is hierarchical; it works on many levels simultaneously. For instance, a C major chord can be the I chord in the key of C major and the V chord in F major at the same time. In the key of C major, a D7 chord is V of V (G) while it bears a II relationship to the I chord (C maj7). The entire concept of modulation relies on this. That is why there can be V of V, V of II, II–V–I of IV, etc. within one composition, while maintaining an ultimate tonic key. Modal music is more one-dimensional; the focus is more on pure melody. Modal performances seem to accumulate more than proceed.

Modes are usually derived from the major scale. All of these modes can be transposed to begin on any note. In chapter 3, the modes related to improvising on chords, each of which generates a scale to use while improvising melodies. In modal music, the opposite is the case; scales can generate chords. For a tune in D Dorian mode, the mode is predetermined, and various chords can be derived and improvised from it.

Modal Chords

Diatonic Seventh Chords

In most modal situations, the pianist is free to play any chords that fall within the mode's framework. Any simultaneous pitch aggregates derived from the mode will "work." Thus, one can play any diatonic seventh chord derived from the mode. Here's an example for D Dorian.

These chords can be voiced in all the ways described in previous chapters for one or two hands.

Quartal Diatonic Chords

One can also derive quartal chords for one or two hands. Here are examples in D Dorian for three, four, five, and six notes.

"So What"

The most-played tune from *Kind of Blue,* "So What," was radical for its time but did not really sound that way. One reason is the beautiful and subtle playing on it; another is that it still contains traditional elements. The form is that of a traditional thirty-two-measure pop song: AABA, with each section lasting eight measures. Instead of chord progressions, each section is governed by a mode: the A sections are in D Dorian, and the B section is in E♭ Dorian. Once the tune has begun, there are twenty-four measures in a row of D Dorian—the last A section plus the first two A sections—before the B section arrives. The B section creates tension by shifting the mode up a half step. That tension is released at the return of the A section.

The famous "So What" voicing used by Bill Evans started a revolution in post bop harmonic practice. The combined quartal-tertial voicing, comprised of two 4ths and a major 3rd, was unique at the time. Note that the voicings are not for any specific chords, but rather for a specific mode, in this case Dorian.

Again, we should be reminded that "sound" is crucial in determining voicings. In a modal setting that lacks predetermined chords and harmonic syntax, the coloristic aspect of a voicing is paramount.

Quartal Clusters

Cluster sounds can be derived from quartal voicings by rearranging the notes to form 2nds. These voicings can offer relief from open quartal voicings while retaining a quartal quality.

Modal Comping

Modal comping is free from predetermined chord changes, but usually employs many different "chords." These chords are derived from the mode, and almost any sound or voicing can be used to imply the mode rather than any particular chord. Below is an example of how a pianist might comp in a D Dorian situation. The sonorities vary among "So What," quartal, tertial, and cluster voicings, all of which come from the mode.

TRACK 2

Modal Improvisation

The concept of *modal improvisation* seems simple on the surface; any notes from the mode will work. While this is true, it is no guarantee of success. The lack of harmonic progression and cadence leaves the improviser with perhaps too much freedom. While one note can seem dynamic and flowing when held over changing harmony, the same held note can seem static and dull in a modal situation. In modal playing, the improviser is forced to think melodically rather than harmonically. Traditional melodic devices, such as sequences, motivic development, and manipulation work well in modal settings.

Patterns

Modal tunes invite pattern playing. *Patterns* are groups of usually two to six notes that are sequenced to form longer lines. They differ from *motives* because they lack any rhythmic definition. They usually contain notes of the same duration, such as all eighth notes or all sixteenth notes, etc. Patterns offer ways of getting around the mode while keeping up rhythmic momentum.

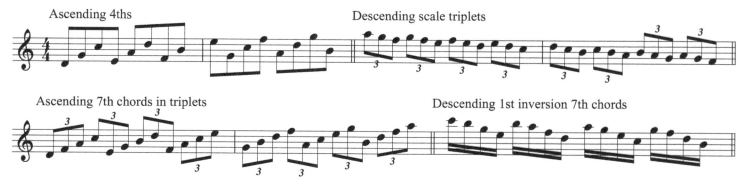

Pentatonic Scales

Players often superimpose pentatonic scales on the prevailing mode. The process is similar to that used when superimposing on a chord. The use of different pentatonic scales on the same mode offers variety in modal coloring by isolating certain tones at the expense of others. Most pentatonic playing is done in modal situations. Below are the three most common pentatonic scales superimposed on a Dorian mode, shown here for D Dorian. These are minor pentatonic scales built from the tonic, second degree, and fifth degree of the mode.

By isolating one of these pentatonic scales for short or long periods of time, the player extracts a mode (scale) from within the mode. If modes can be thought of as colors, these inner pentatonic scales can be thought of as different tints of those colors. Theorists have described these particular pentatonic scales used on Dorian in terms of most "inside" and most "outside." The minor pentatonic scale from D (tonic) seems to be more firmly rooted in the tonic modality, the scale from E (second degree) much less so, and the scale from A (fifth degree) somewhere in between. See Chapters 7 and 8 on McCoy Tyner and Chick Corea for examples of pentatonic superimposition in modal contexts.

Melodic Fourths

Fourths are used melodically as well as harmonically in modal playing. The relationship between fourths and pentatonic scales becomes apparent in much modal playing. McCoy Tyner and Chick Corea, among others, have amply explored this relationship. The notes of a traditional pentatonic scale can be rearranged into a series of perfect 4ths.

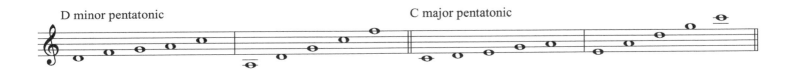

Many modal melodies are made of 4ths, many of them from pentatonic scales. Below is a typical modal melody built around 4ths in F Dorian.

Four-Note Melodic Cells

Post bop players often isolated groupings of notes and sequenced them both in and out of the prevailing key or mode. Often these groupings, or *cells*, are derived from pentatonic scales. The extracted *four-note cells* serve as patterns from which to construct improvised melodies. Four-note pentatonic cells derived from the C major (or A minor) pentatonic scale are shown below.

The notes of these cells can be played in any order while the cell itself is transposed to other pitch levels. The following line uses the same four-note cell throughout, transposed from C to D and back to C major pentatonic.

Side-Slipping

Jazz musicians often play outside the mode temporarily. This is known as *side-slipping*. It is usually done by raising or lowering the mode, scale, or chord by a half step. This happens most often in modal settings, but the technique is used also in tonal environments. Four-note cells are often used in these situations. The next example demonstrates side-slipping and left-hand modal voicings during a typical modal improvisation in D Dorian. Side-slipping offers a way to relieve the monotony of the mode and a way of creating *tension and relief*.

TRACK 3

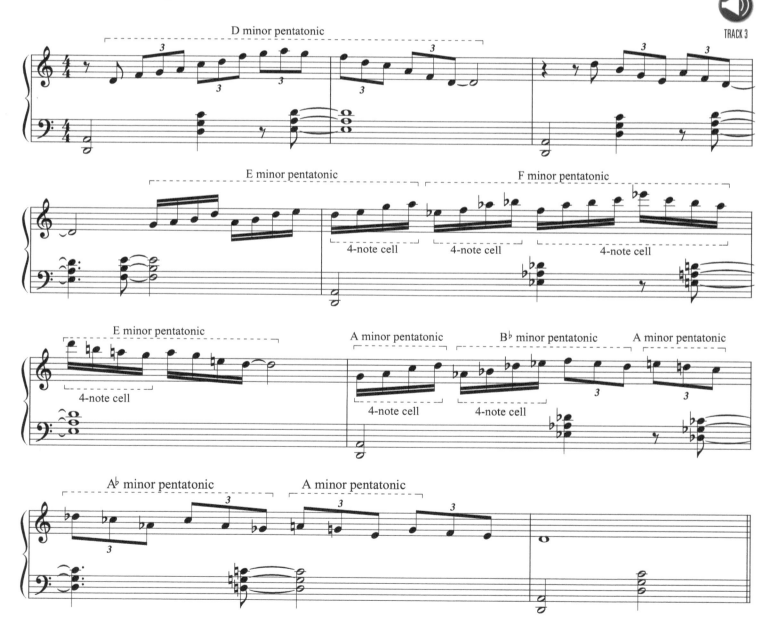

Modalization

Modalization refers to the process of superimposing modal attributes upon an otherwise non-modal framework. It is one of the hallmarks of post bop jazz. Modalization can be done melodically and/or harmonically. The whole concept of deriving scales from chords is a form of modalization, but true modalization occurs when conventions of consonance and dissonance in relation to a chord are ignored at the expense of modal melody. One can generally modalize in three ways:

1) Select a single mode to play over changing chords. In this example, the right hand plays on a D minor pentatonic scale extracted from B♭ Ionian (major), against a II–V–I progression in B♭ major.

2) Select a single mode to superimpose on a chord progression. Here the right hand plays from the chord changes while the left hand treats the scale of the key of F major as an Ionian mode.

3) Treat both hands modally. In this example, side-slipping is used in both hands.

CHAPTER 5

BILL EVANS

Post bop piano begins fully with Bill Evans' playing during the late 1950s. He remains the most influential pianist of the post-bop era. Almost all pianists after him have incorporated at least some of his innovations. A brief list of his most important innovations follows.

- Systematized and explored the use of rootless voicings

- Used chord voicings as tone colors

- Used fragments for chord voicings

- Used quartal voicings

- Pioneered the use of modal jazz

- Used scales and modes for improvisation and compositions

- Developed ideas during improvisations

- Used the damper pedal often

- Developed a new way to play block chords

- Pioneered the concept of rhythm-section interplay along with Scott LaFaro and Paul Motian

Evans was a major contributor to the Miles Davis album, *Kind of Blue*. His pioneering trio with Scott LaFaro and Paul Motian demonstrated that jazz could be freer without being "free" (à la Ornette Coleman). This group leads directly to the freewheeling Miles Davis rhythm section of the 1960s with Herbie Hancock, Ron Carter, and Tony Williams. Practically all of the post bop characteristics described in the previous chapters of this book relate to the originality, artistry, and innovations of Bill Evans.

Melodic Ideas

Bill Evans developed an original approach to improvisation based on the development and evolution of *ideas*. An idea usually consists of a grouping of notes that have a distinct melodic and rhythmic character. This is commonly referred to as a *motive*. Some ideas can be just rhythmic or intervallic in character. *Motivic development* in jazz was not new with Evans, but he used the technique in unique ways, developing an organic method of evolving or growing new material from previously played material.

Motives

Here is an Evans-esque improvised melody based on the interval of a descending 5th. Each statement of the idea or motive (a) descends stepwise, creating a connecting step-wise basic (or long-range) pitch motion (indicated by asterisks). (This type of long-range step-wise connection will be indicated throughout the book.)

TRACK 7
(meas. 1—4)

Motivic Development

In a latter version of the same tune, Evans again develops a motive, but now the motive and process are more complex. He breaks the motive into component parts and recombines them to form a melody. The entire motive and its components are analyzed below.

Notice in the following full excerpt how the basic pitch line descends stepwise, and the original idea is fragmented and reassembled in an interesting and unpredictable manner. Also, notice the (b1) motive in the third and fourth measures. The triplet rhythm is slightly changed, and a typical Evans neighbor note figure is inserted in the middle. This demonstrates Evans's subtlety and compositional/organic approach to improvisation.

TRACK 8

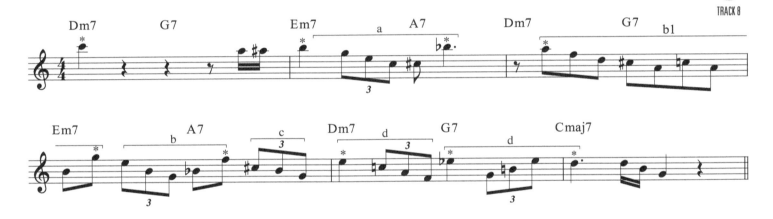

The next excerpt develops and evolves the original idea of a leap up and back to the starting note (a) in subtle and interesting ways.

TRACK 9

Rhythmic Displacement and Variation

Evans often kept the pitch element of a motive while changing its rhythm parameters. This example rhythmically manipulates a simple motive based on a descending scale. The whole segment is organized within a descending basic pitch line.

TRACK 10

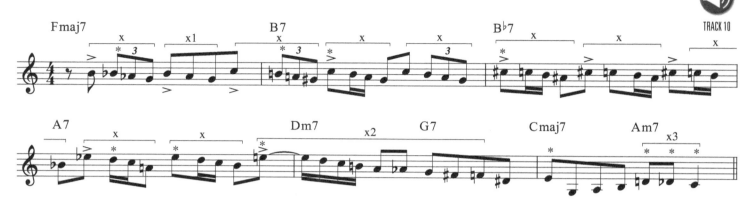

Organic Evolution

This example uses a motive and combines it with several new ideas. After the opening (a) motive comes (c), (d), and (e) in order. Then (e) begins to "grow" with each restatement after (e1). After a reappearance of (c) and (d), (e) re-emerges in a chromatic form as a dominant diminished scale, getting even longer and higher. After a descending motion that includes the (d) idea, (e) grows still larger as a dominant diminished scale. After a descending line, (a1) ends the segment.

TRACK 11

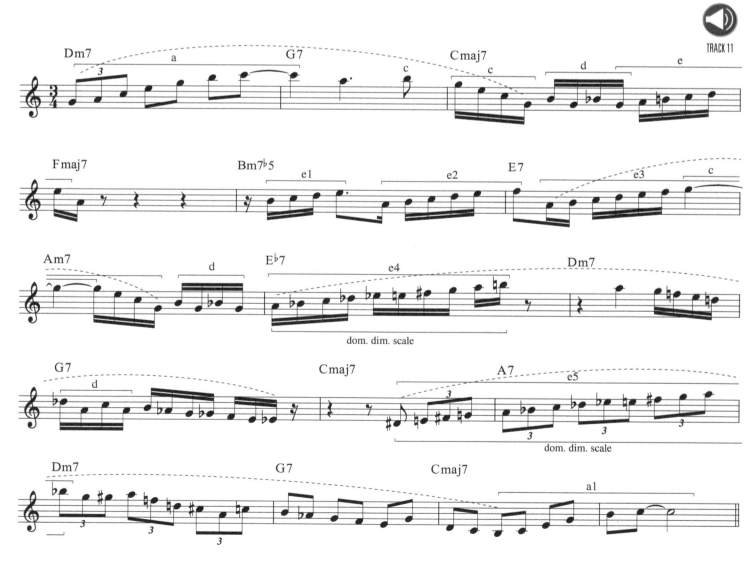

Arches

There is another idea at work in the previous example that is common to all phases of Bill Evans's career: the shaping of phrases into *arches*, indicated by the dotted lines. These "waves" of notes create a rhythm and sense of drama all their own. Notice how he resolves the tension of the segment with the reappearance of the diatonic (a) idea.

Sequences

Evans often sequenced melodic fragments. In the following example, three statements of a melodic idea are played on different pitch levels. The first two statements are identical, but the third is changed slightly. Notice how each statement begins in a different spot of the measure. Notice also the mini arch shapes.

TRACK 12

This example elaborates on a sequence by transforming the idea each time. Notice the arches and how the last statement is stretched out.

TRACK 13

Motivic Transformation

Evans also used *motivic transformation* in his solos. This occurs when a motive is gradually developed and changed into a new motive. In the example below, Evans develops and distorts his initial idea into a new idea. The opening interval of a 5th in (a) is changed to a 7th in (a1) and is filled in at (a2). The last note is changed in (a3) and moves up by step instead of down by a 3rd. A downward octave leap is added to the end of (a3), and while this can be thought of as (a4), it has been changed so much from the initial motive that we also can call it (b). The (b) motive is then shortened to form (b1), and then distorted slightly to form (b2).

TRACK 14

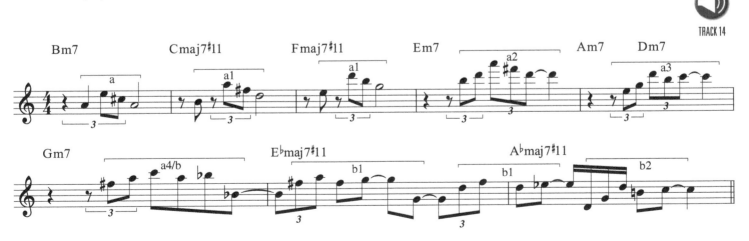

Repeated Notes and Figures

Often, Evans would repeat a note or interval to produce an interesting rhythmic effect. Notice the cross-rhythmic effect shown below. Notice also the coloristic effect of the repeated pitch over changing harmony.

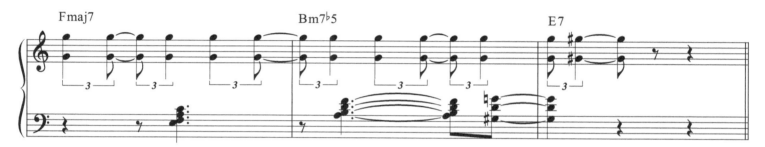

Varied Repetition

Evans often played similar lines on reoccurring chord changes during a particular tune. In an AABA form, for example, he might play similar material for the first four measures of each A section, for a chorus or more. The excerpt below shows several variations on a similar section of the tune.

Local Ideas

Local ideas are short ideas that seem to arrive spontaneously and spawn instant variations of themselves. Local ideas differ from motives in that they are purely local in effect and embedded in the general flow of a melodic line (rather than isolated or related to long-term ideas). The following example spins out the descending three-note stepwise idea from the first measure into the succeeding two measures. The idea is twice inverted (x1), and then extended (x2) in the second measure.

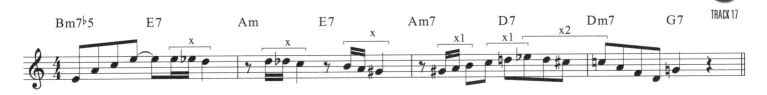

Interior Motives

Interior motives are patterns of notes that are sequenced and connected to form longer lines. In this example, a sequential-like line is spun from the opening idea.

Rhythmic Ideas

Bill Evans often developed rhythmic ideas with both hands, sometimes playing one hand off the other. In the example below, the right hand plays the first two notes, and the left plays the third note of repeating triplets, creating a call-and-response effect.

Cross Rhythms

Evans often superimposed a *cross rhythm* or other meter against the prevailing meter, creating polyrhythmic or polymetric effects. Here he plays a triple jazz waltz cross rhythm over the quadruple meter.

TRACK 20

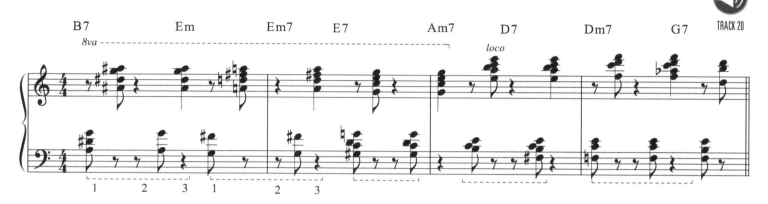

In the next excerpt, he superimposes a duple meter over the original triple meter.

TRACK 21

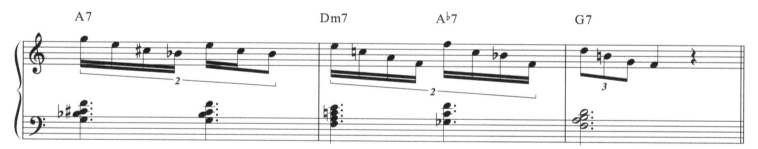

MELODIC DEVICES

Characteristic Figure

Bill Evans often played a figure characterized by a descending chromatic motion that alternates with a repeated note. The intervals usually involve 3rds, or 3rds and 2nds. The effect here is to continue a rhythmic motion (eighth notes, sixteenth notes, etc.) while delaying the chromatic motion. Three examples follow.

TRACK 22

Arpeggios

Evans often used arpeggios in his melodic lines. They consisted of lower and upper chord tones. He often played bebop-like figures and lines but disguised them in various ways. The ascending arpeggio preceded by a stepwise motion was a staple of the bebop style; notice its use in the previous example. While bebop players used the stepwise pickup as more of an upbeat or anacrusis to a beat, Evans started the prefix on the beat more often than not.

Notice in this excerpt how these bebop-like figures sound very unlike bebop in this context. Notice also the descending arpeggio motions indicated below the staff.

TRACK 23

Evans constructed many of his lines in 3rds or primarily 3rds. Here is an example in typical Evans fashion; an ascending diatonic line in 3rds is followed by a descending diatonic motion in 3rds, forming an arch. The descending motion is then continued with a chromatically inflected scalar motion that resolves to a mostly diatonic melody based on lower chord tones.

TRACK 24

Left-Hand Techniques

Rhythmic Unison

Bill Evans invented a new way to play block chords. The technique is quite simple; the right hand plays single-note lines while the left plays a chord voicing with each right-hand note. In actual practice, the left hand plays along with most (but not necessarily all) of the right-hand notes. This technique ingeniously combines the best of two worlds: the rich texture and colors of block chords, including locked hands techniques, are preserved while the right hand is free to play quick, articulated, and expressive lines. As in other block chord techniques, each melody note is colored by the left-hand voicing. Naturally for Evans, these voicing are usually rootless. Three examples follow.

TRACK 25

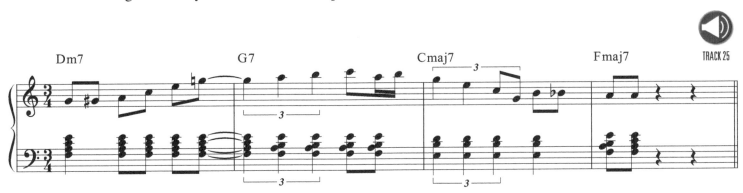

Comping

Evans comped in various ways. Sometimes the left hand operated on a plane all its own, while at other times it worked with or off the right hand. He would sometimes integrate the left and right hands to create various rhythmic patterns and/or ideas.

Evans would sometimes comp using a consistent rhythmic pattern. He would do this for only brief periods—never much more than eight measures. The following excerpt demonstrates consistent rhythmic comping on the "ands" of beats 2 and 4. This sets the anticipation of beats 1 and 3 and is reminiscent of Ahmad Jamal's and Red Garland's comping approach. Notice the typical Evans arch in the right-hand line.

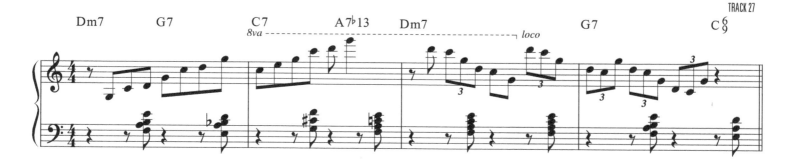

Here the left hand reinforces accents in the right-hand line from the end of the second measure on.

The next excerpt shows an example of the left hand working off the right-hand line. Here the left hand compliments the right hand and fills the gaps for the shortened motive.

Chords with Two Hands

Block Chords

Sometimes Evans played passages using the locked hands technique. In this example, the left hand doubles the top note an octave below.

Here is an example of how Evans used the drop 2 technique.

From time to time, Evans played melodies with full chords in both hands.

Comping with Two Hands

Evans used most of the voicings described earlier in this book when he comped for someone else. He freely combined root with rootless, open with closed, and quartal with tertial. Notice the variety of sound and texture in this excerpt behind a bass solo.

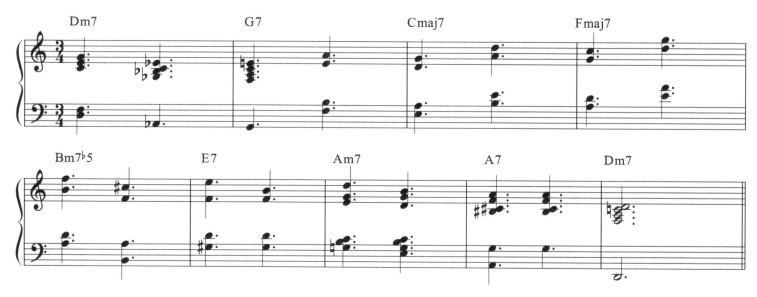

This is a tune and improvisation inspired by Bill Evans.

IN SEARCH OF LOST TIME

TRACK 33

John Valerio

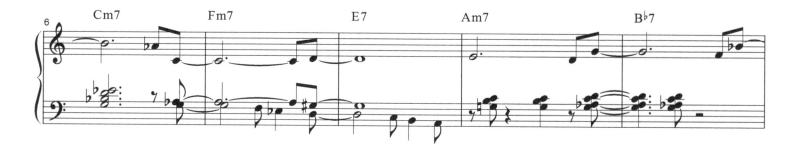

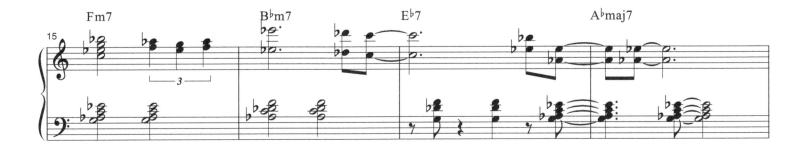

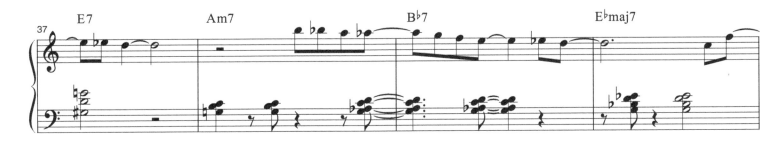

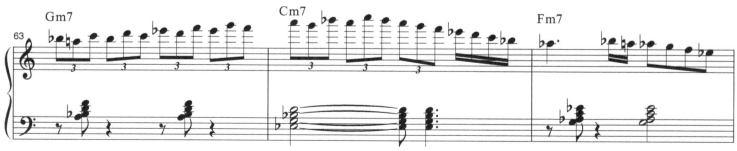

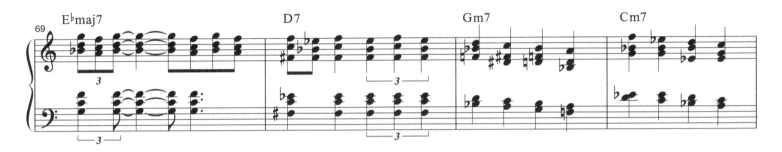

Chapter 6
HERBIE HANCOCK

Herbie Hancock developed an original style derived in part from Bill Evans and Wynton Kelly, the two pianists that preceded him in Miles Davis's band. He employed many of Evans's voicings as well as his scale approach. Hancock's buoyant touch and blues-like colorations were like Kelly's. Hancock ventured into many areas, including fusion, free jazz, and pop, but his post bop style of the 1960s will be the focus here. While with the Miles Davis band during the 1960s, Hancock was a member of what many consider the greatest rhythm section of all time, including Ron Carter on bass and Tony Williams on drums. He set the standard for post bop comping that could be sensitive or aggressive, flowing or rhythmic. He was instrumental in developing a post bop composition style as well as a piano style.

Melodic Ideas

Motives

Hancock often exploited motives in his playing, many of which seem to arrive from nowhere and take on lives of their own. They usually evolve into repetitive riff-like figures that have a clearly defined pitch and rhythmic character. In this excerpt he seems to stumble upon an idea based on a descending 3rd that he turns it into a groove-based riff.

TRACK 34

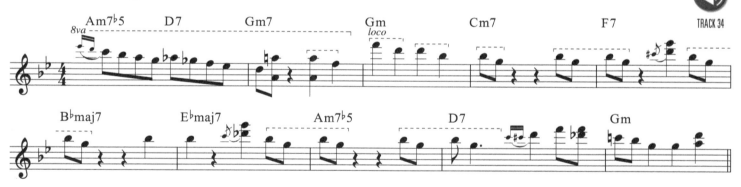

The next example shows another favorite Hancock device: creating a riff-like motive but subtly varying the rhythm each time. Notice how the original idea (a) gets turned into (a1) by changing the last note from a descending leap to an ascending leap. The two versions then alternate in a call and response-like manner.

TRACK 35

The following example shows how Hancock turns a vague idea based on 4ths and 5ths into a clearly defined motive whose last notes get higher each time. The passage ends with a bebop-like line, in typical Hancock fashion. Notice the ascending basic pitch motion (marked by asterisks).

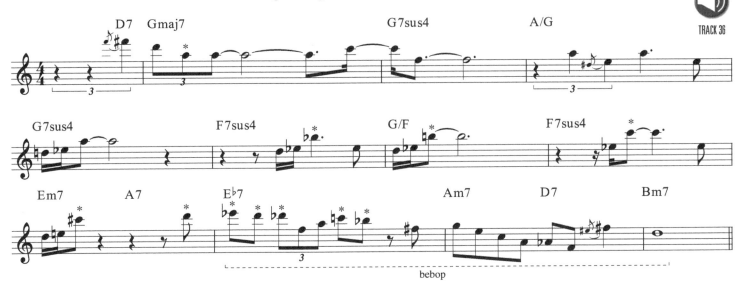

Varied Repetition

The next example shows how Hancock develops a blues riff by varying each repetition. Notice the way he emphasizes certain notes with octaves in the beginning and other intervals toward the end.

Sequenced Patterns and Interior Motives

Hancock often sequenced patterns (interior motives) to form longer lines. Here Hancock sequences a simple descending whole-step pattern by playing it a half step lower each time. This sequence is interrupted briefly by a chromatic line during the second measure.

Hancock often played pattern runs reminiscent of Art Tatum. This example shows a repetitive triplet pattern sequenced a 3rd higher each time.

TRACK 39

Hancock often sequenced arpeggio patterns. In the following example, he plays upper structure arpeggios with added notes beginning with Em/G7, Am/C7, etc.

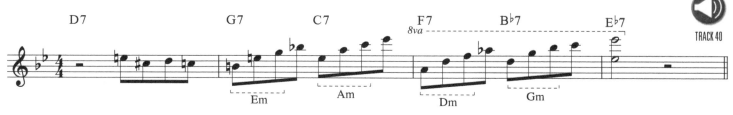

TRACK 40

Sequenced Lines

Hancock often sequenced longer lines with variations. This example shows two sequenced variations on the first idea. Notice the triplet pattern in the first two statements. The third statement follows the same motion as the others, but lacks the inner sequential triplet idea.

TRACK 41

MELODIC DEVICES

Blues

Herbie Hancock often flavored his solos with blues licks and blue notes derived from the blues scale. Three excerpts follow.

TRACK 42

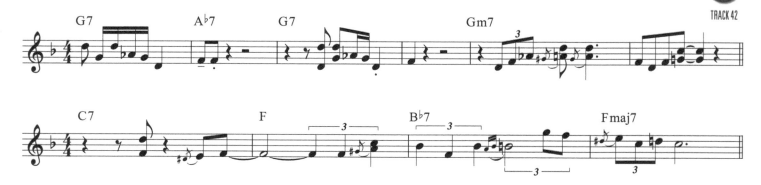

Octaves

Hancock often interspersed octaves among his single-note lines. The use of octaves gives these notes special emphasis within the melodic line. Two examples follow.

TRACK 43

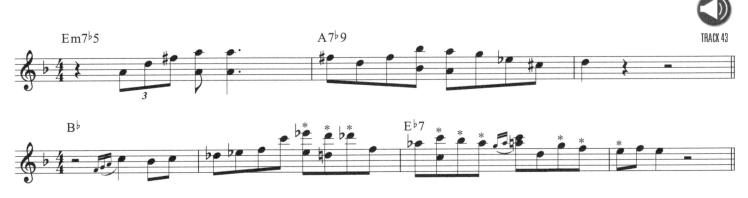

Altered Scales

Hancock used modern scales frequently. He often colored his dominant chords with altered scales. This example has altered scales switching for each dominant chord.

TRACK 44

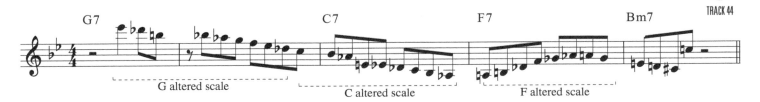

Dominant Diminished Scales

Hancock also made use of the dominant diminished (half-whole) scale on dominant chords.

TRACK 45

Arpeggios

Hancock often thought in upper-structure polychordal formations. He used them most often as superimposed arpeggios. This example follows the Cm9 arpeggio with arpeggios based on C/Eb7, Cb/Ab7, and Dm/G7.

TRACK 46

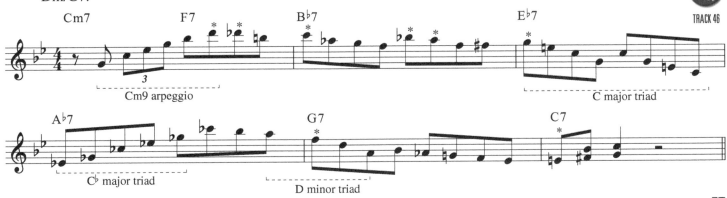

Left-Hand Comping

Hancock voiced chords and comped in the left hand much like Bill Evans. He preferred two-, three-, and four-note rootless voicings. In this example, the random-like nature of the left-hand comping gives impetus to the right-hand line and supplies tension and variety to the repetitive right-hand blues lick.

TRACK 47

In this excerpt he plays a more consistent left-hand rhythm à la Red Garland. Notice the chord and upper structure arpeggios, as well as the basic pitch motion indicated by (∗).

TRACK 48

Chords with Two Hands

Block Chords

Hancock often played solos with two-hand chording. These chords usually consisted of left-hand rootless voicings and right-hand quartal structures, upper structures, or filled-in octaves. He often repeated these chords in very distinct, emphatic rhythms.

Comping with Two Hands

All of the voicings shown above are typical of the voicings Hancock used for comping. Below are voicings and rhythmic characteristics that are typical of his post-bop comping. These bright and clear voicings work well with an aggressive rhythm section.

Suspended Chords and Vamps

Hancock pioneered the use of suspended chords in post bop jazz. The neutral sound and ambiguous tonal leanings of these chords lent themselves to the modal and quasi-modal world of 1960s jazz. Hancock had a knack for inventing infectious rhythmic vamps.

59

Here is a tune and improvisation influenced by Herbie Hancock.

DELPHIC DALLIANCE

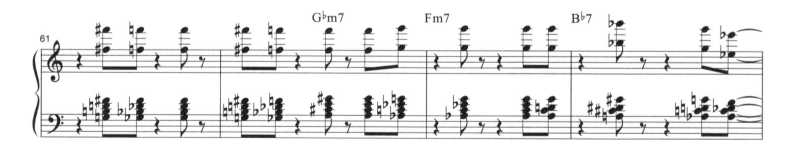

Chapter 7

McCOY TYNER

Although Miles Davis and Bill Evans began the use of modes in jazz, it was John Coltrane and McCoy Tyner who evolved the concept during the 1960s. Tyner along with Jimmy Garrison on bass and Elvin Jones on drums played in Coltrane's Classic Quartet from the early to mid 1960s. His unique harmonic, melodic, and rhythmic style was a perfect compliment to Coltrane's free-wheeling modal explorations and Jones's polyrhythmic drumming.

Left-Hand Voicings and Modalization

Left-Hand Voicings

McCoy Tyner used standard and rootless voicings in some of his playing but is more known for using quartal left-hand voicings. In pure modal environments, he often shifted three-note quartal chords around the mode while randomly emphasizing the roots by playing low-register open 5ths.

TRACK 52

Left-Hand Modalization

Tyner modalized nearly everything he played. He did this with both melodies and chords. For example, a C7 chord represents a C Mixolydian mode (C–D–E–F–G–A–B♭). His comping chords are usually shifting within the mode, and any chord or voicing that contains notes from the mode can be representative of the given chord. This example shows how he freely played chords derived from the implied scales (modes) of the chords, rather than just playing voicings of the chords. Notice the G minor triad stressed during the Fm7 chord.

TRACK 53

Melodic Devices

Modal Patterns

Tyner developed a technique inspired by Coltrane that grouped notes into patterns. Each pattern served as a unit, and each unit took the place of one note. Tyner often played patterns that lie under moving hand positions. These note patterns were usually played very fast with consistent durations, such as all eighth notes or all sixteenth notes. Therefore, these patterns have no motivic value since they are rhythmically nondescript and are used from solo to solo. This example demonstrates similar but non-repetitive patterns running through an E Phrygian mode.

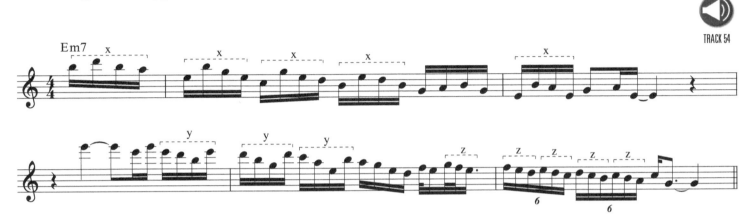

Right-Hand Modalization

Tyner modalized nearly all of his melodic material. Here he treats the dominant chords, C7 and F7, as two Mixolydian modes. Notice the quasi-recurring patterns and the modal-like left-hand playing.

Pentatonic Scales

Tyner made frequent use of pentatonic scales. He freely superimposes them onto existing scale and modes. This example uses a B♭ Mixolydian mode on the B♭7 chord, then a B♭ minor (D♭ major) pentatonic scale on both E♭7 and B♭7. Notice again the quasi-recurring patterns and modalized left-hand chords.

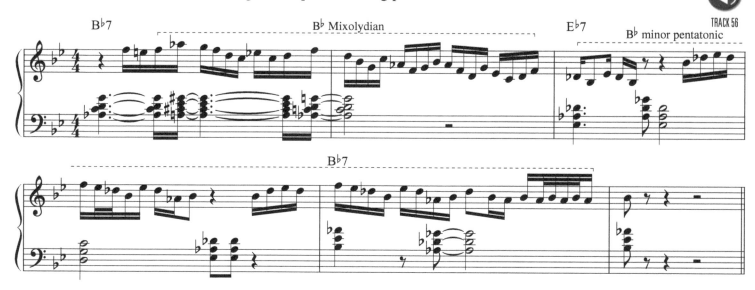

Side-Slipping

Tyner uses side-slipping extensively in modal and non-modal tunes. He typically starts a phrase with an inside tonality, slips to an outside tonality, then slips back to an inside tonality. This example starts within an F Mixolydian mode, then slips to a G♭ major pentatonic, and then comes back to F Mixolydian. Notice how the C minor pentatonic is extracted from within the F Mixolydian at the end.

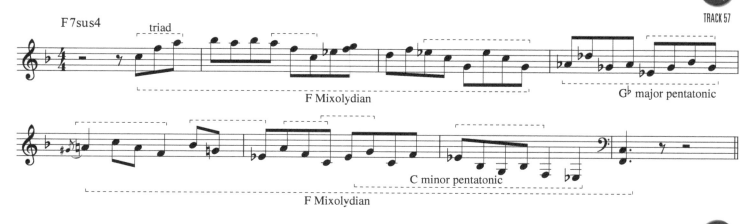

Here he slips above and below the prevailing G minor tonality with both hands.

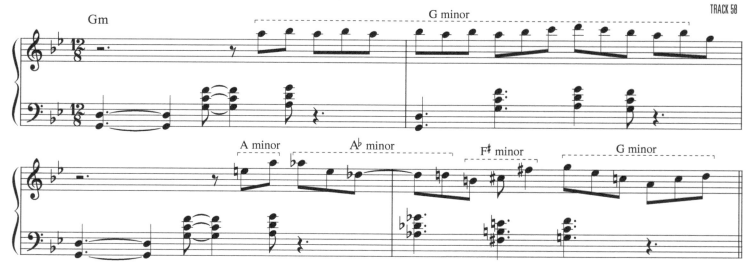

Repeated Patterns and Four-Note Cells

Tyner often played repeated patterns in the right hand while moving quartal voicings in the left hand. Here he repeats a four-note cell that could be derived from a G blues scale, while the left hand ascends in quartal chords.

TRACK 59

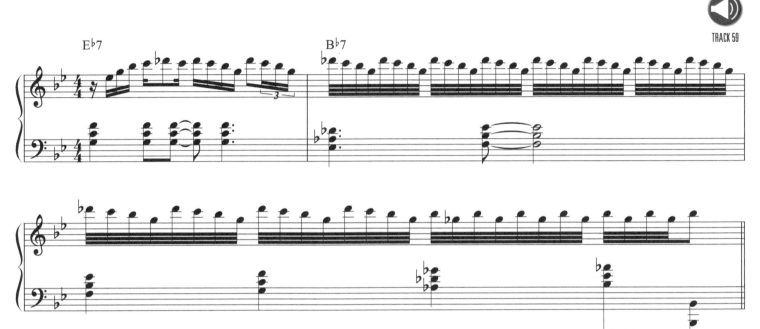

This next example superimposes a 3/4 cross meter on the underlying 4/4 by repeating a pattern characterized by 4ths and based on a B♭ minor (D♭ major) pentatonic scale.

TRACK 60

Tyner often takes four-note cells and plays the notes in a random-like order. In this example, he does so while superimposing a 3/8 cross rhythm by playing almost continuous dotted quarter notes in the left hand. The first cell (x) is very dissonant against the left hand, and the second (y) resolves the tension.

TRACK 61

Chords with Two Hands

Chord Melody

Sometimes Tyner extended the left-hand quartal voicings to four notes and played them with both hands, resulting in melodies played in *parallel 4ths*.

TRACK 62

Here a repetitive pattern is voiced in 4ths in the right hand while the left hand plays random-like parallel quartal chords against it.

TRACK 63

Voicings and Comping for Two Hands

Tyner sometimes played rich, full tertial voicings while comping. He could establish strong overtones by playing open 5ths in the low register with his left hand while playing closed-position voicings in the right hand. At times he played the closed-position voicings in the left hand while playing octaves in the right hand, to produce a bell-like ringing sound. He often used four-, five-, and six-note quartal voicings in both hands but also superimposed two sets of three-note quartal voicings on each other to produce a variety of sounds.

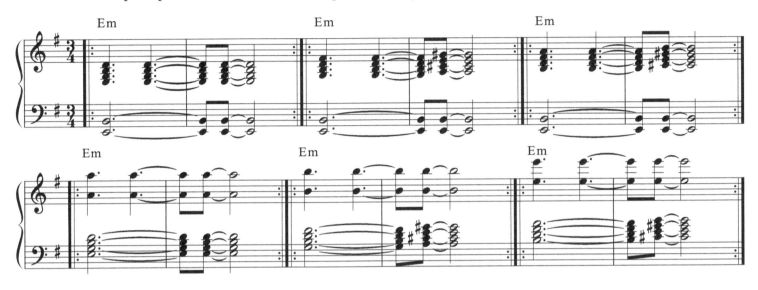

Here, quartal as well as tertial voicings are played with upper structures.

Here is a tune and improvisation inspired by McCoy Tyner.

SOLSTICE

John Valerio

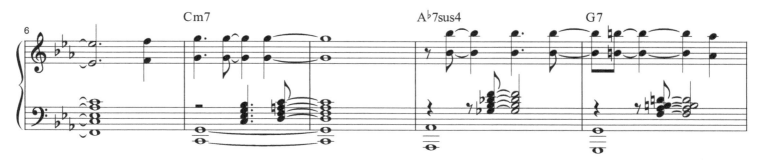

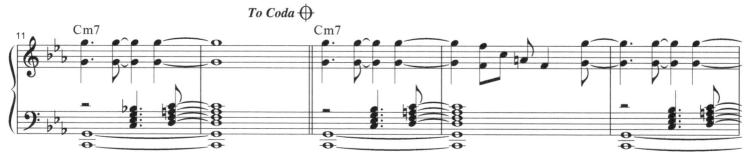

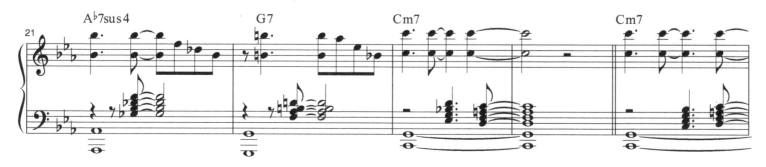

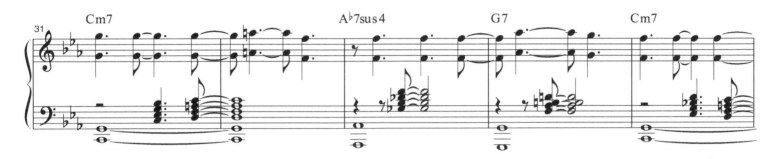

D.C. al Coda

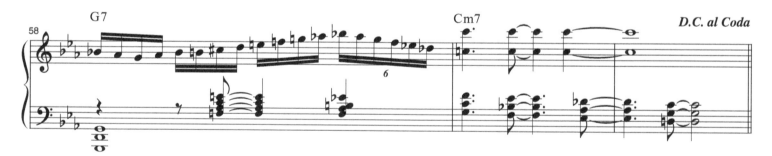

⊕ *Coda*

Chapter 8
CHICK COREA

Chick Corea emerged during the 1960s as a promising young pianist while playing as a sideman with various groups and began recording under his own name in 1966. After playing with Miles Davis for a few years beginning in 1969, he mostly led his own groups. He originally played somewhat like Bill Evans, but later developed a right-hand and left-hand style partly derived from McCoy Tyner's playing. He made much use of pentatonic scales and quartal voicings. Like Herbie Hancock, Corea also ventured into free jazz and fusion; his group Return to Forever explored new ways of incorporating Latin music into the jazz world. The focus here will be on his post bop style.

Left-Hand Voicings and Comping

Corea mostly used quartal or open three-note voicings in his left hand. Occasionally he would use standard rootless voicings and fragments. Although he favored the modal approach, his left hand was generally lighter and rhythmically more supple than McCoy Tyner's.

TRACK 65

Melodic Devices

Pentatonic Scales

Chick Corea made much use of pentatonic scales in modal and non-modal contexts. Here he creates a melodic arch by superimposing an F minor pentatonic scale over a B♭ Dorian mode on a B♭m7 chord.

TRACK 66

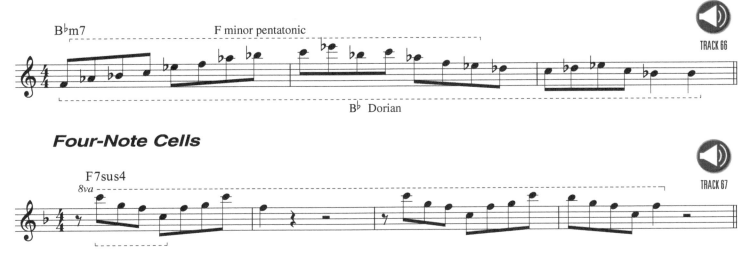

Four-Note Cells

TRACK 67

Corea derived four-note cells (see Chapter 3) from pentatonic scales. In this excerpt, he plays a simple repetitive figure based on a four-note cell derived from a B♭ or E♭ major pentatonic scale.

Here he derives two different four-note cells from the same C minor pentatonic scale: C–E♭–F–B♭ and C–E♭–G–B♭. Notice the circular repetition of the notes. He follows the two pentatonic cells with a chromatic line that leads to a diatonic Mixolydian segment that resolves the preceding tension.

TRACK 68

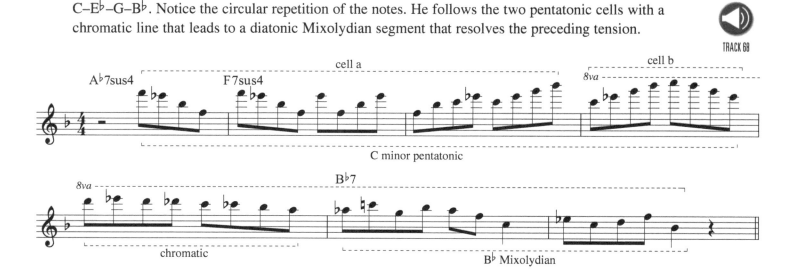

In this excerpt he manipulates a non-pentatonic cell with varying rhythms.

TRACK 69

Interior Motives

Corea often constructed longer lines from short interior motives that combined with other interior motives. Interior motives are groupings of usually three or four notes of equal duration that outline a certain interval/ shape pattern. They can be played in their original formation, in retrograde (r), or can be sequenced to any pitch. Here he manipulates two different interior motives within two different pentatonic scales.

TRACK 70

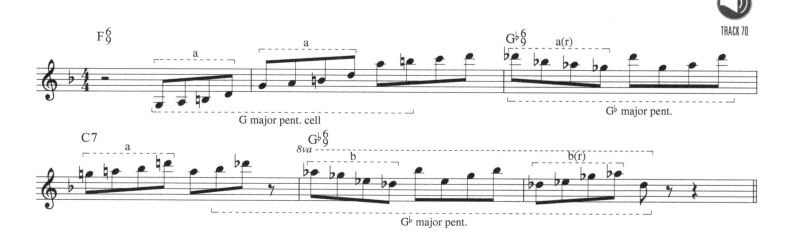

In this excerpt, three different four-note interior motives make up almost the entire segment. Corea adeptly transitions from a dominant diminished (half-whole) scale to a whole-tone scale to a Dorian mode to several different pentatonic cells.

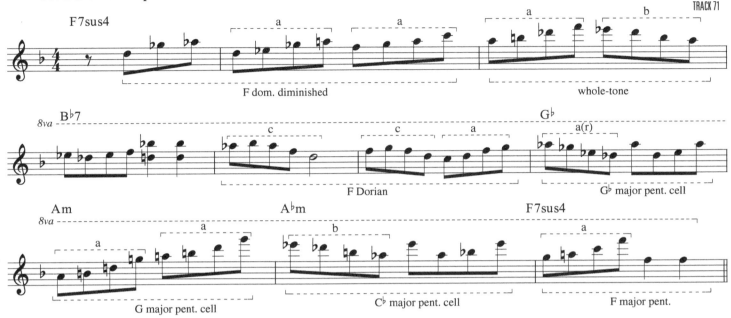

Upper Structure Arpeggios

Corea used many arpeggio patterns in his playing. These usually involved upper structures or polychords. Here he superimposes a D°7 arpeggio over an F7#9 chord and a C major triad over a Bb7 chord. Notice how the left-hand comping articulates the right-hand line.

Several upper structure arpeggios are used in this excerpt.

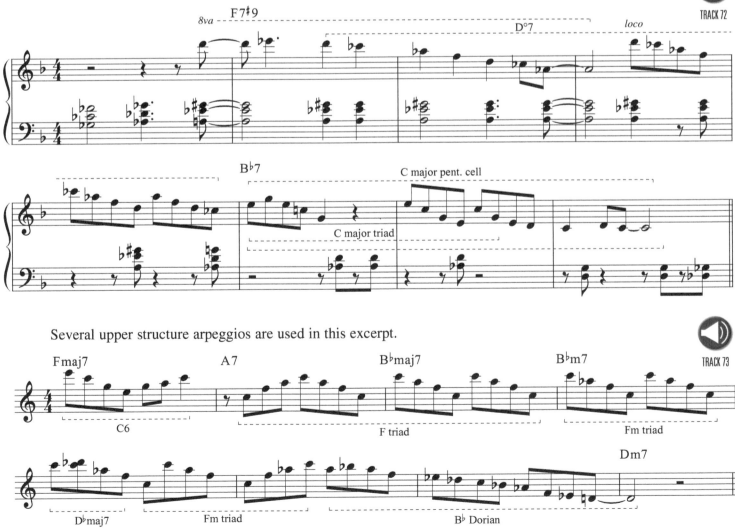

Corea liked to superimpose a consistent repeating triad arpeggio over changing chords. This example shows him playing around with an E major triad arpeggio over four different chords.

TRACK 74

Motives

Clear-cut motives appear in Corea's playing, and he frequently develops them with varied repetitions. This example shows how he makes gradual changes with each appearance of the motive.

TRACK 75

Here Corea plays the initial idea plus three sequential variations derived from four-note pentatonic cells. This is followed by an upper structure arpeggio and a four-note cell—both derived from an F major pentatonic scale. Notice the repeated figure at the end.

TRACK 76

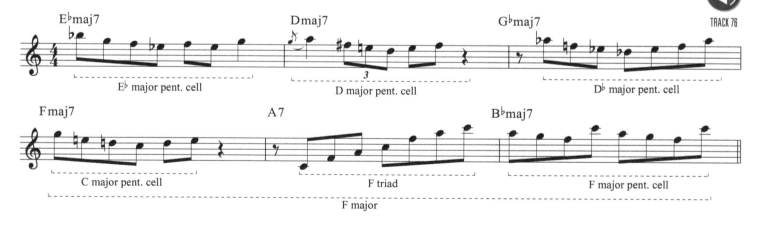

Cross Rhythms

Corea often used cross-rhythmic effects in his melodic lines, superimposing triple on duple or quadruple meter, or quadruple on triple meter, etc. In the following excerpt, twos and fours are superimposed against threes, and threes against twos. Notice the use of an E major pentatonic scale throughout the entire passage; this shows Corea's like for maintaining a consistent scale in the right-hand melodies against changing harmonies in the left hand. This excerpt includes subtle variations on the initial statement. Two versions of a two-note motive (a) are coupled to form a larger motive (aa). After a variation on (aa), we overlap another variant of (aa) with a continuation, (a1).

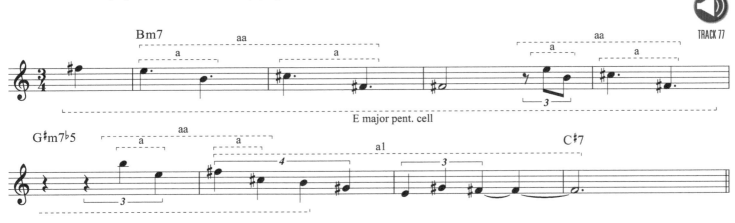

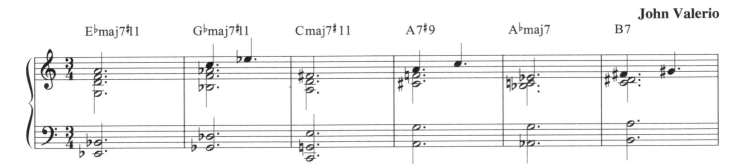

This is a tune and improvisation based on the style of Chick Corea.

PORTALS

John Valerio

To Coda ⊕

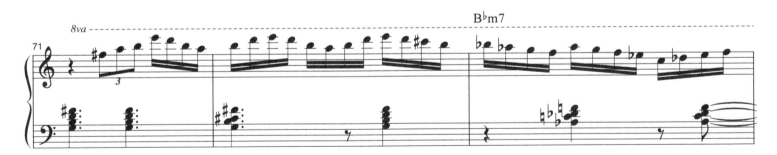

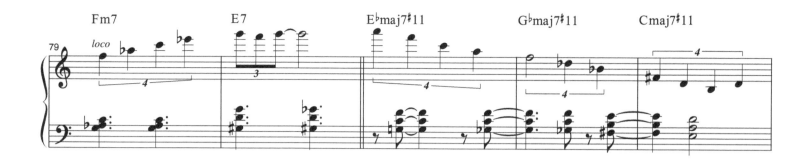

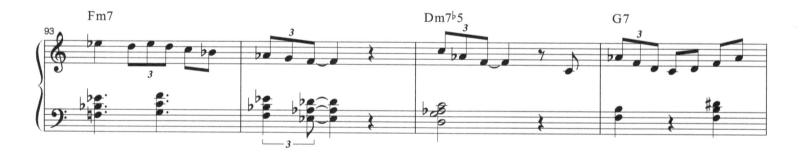

Chapter 9

KEITH JARRETT

Keith Jarrett rose to prominence during the 1960s when he played with Charles Lloyd's quartet. He had a brief stint with Miles Davis in 1970–71, and has since performed solo or with his own groups. Jarrett resurrected the art of jazz solo piano during the 1970s. His original style seems to be a mixture of Bill Evans, bebop, gospel, blues, modal, free jazz, and classical music. His solo performances are usually long, spontaneous improvisations that defy categorization. The trio he formed in 1983 with Gary Peacock on bass and Jack DeJohnette on drums is one of the longest lasting and most remarkable trios in jazz history. With this group, Jarrett brought the *pop standard* back from obscurity. Jarrett's playing style with this trio will be focused on here.

Melodic Ideas

Motivic Development and Transformation

Jarrett continually deals with *motivic development* and *transformation*, as did Bill Evans. This example continually spins out material from an initial statement (a). A new idea (b) is tacked on in measure 7, and this motive grows along with the first idea. The asterisk (*) indicates reference to the main pitches of the theme.

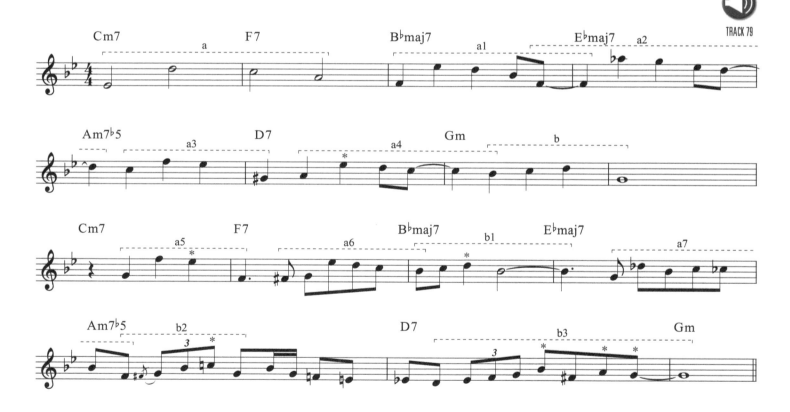

Thematic Reference

Keith Jarrett often bases his improvisations on *thematic reference*, the process of constructing melodic lines either directly from or around key notes from the tune's given melody. The lines are then directed by the tune's melody as much as by its harmonic structure. As opposed to *thematic development*, which develops melodic ideas from the tune (theme), thematic reference refers to the theme's structure on a background, abstract level. While other players have engaged in this practice periodically, Jarrett does it on a much more consistent basis.

In the following example, the key (important) pitches from the given melody are indicated on the top staff, and the improvisation is on the bottom staff. Dotted lines show the relationship between the two. Some points are more obvious than others, but anyone who knows this tune cannot help but hear the references.

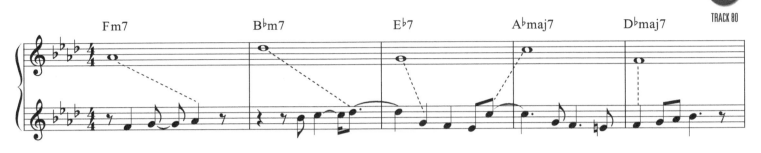

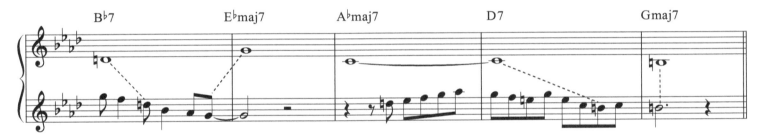

Local Ideas and Sequences

Jarrett often uses local ideas that seem to arise spontaneously. He often plays them with varied repetition and/or sequences. Here are some examples:

In this excerpt from the same tune, he repeats his first idea, plays a sequenced variation of it, and then plays an exact sequence of it with two added notes preceding.

Remote Ideas

Jarrett often picks up on ideas that he played previously during a solo. In this example, he picks up on a triplet idea (a) nine measures later. He extends the idea in a triplet line (a1), then plays a stretched-out version (a2) at the end.

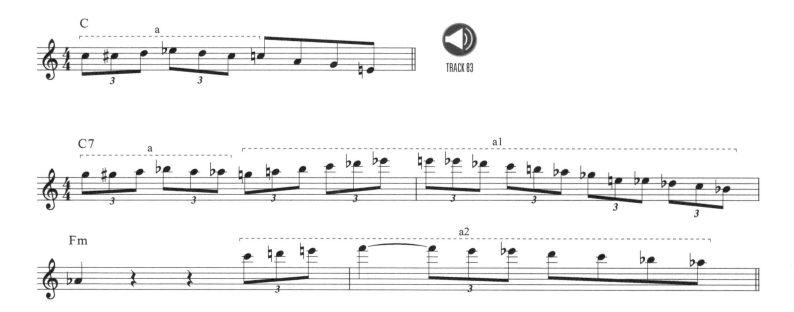

TRACK 83

Melodic Devices

Interior Motives

Jarrett often constructs longer lines from interior motives. Two examples follow.

TRACK 84

Blues

Jarrett often infused his improvisations with blues flavorings. Here blues-like figures are played in an otherwise non-blues setting.

TRACK 85

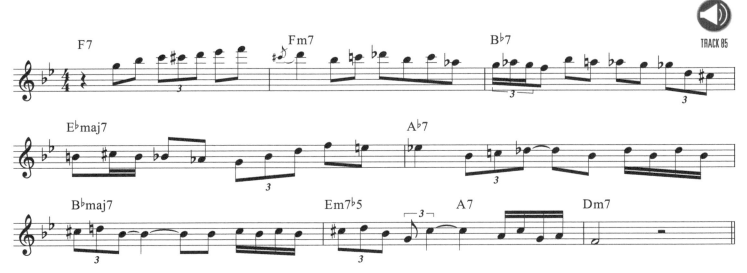

Left-Hand Voicings and Comping

Jarrett favors closed and clustered sounds over the open and quartal sound of McCoy Tyner and Chick Corea. He uses standard rootless voicings, but also plays versions of them with roots clustered into the voicing. Sometimes he played triads with added 9ths.

Comping

Jarrett, at times, can play for long stretches with very little or no left-hand comping, while at other times he can play with a full left-hand compliment. Here is an example of the latter.

TRACK 86

This is a tune and improvisation in the style of Keith Jarrett.

FORGOTTEN MEMORIES

TRACK 87

John Valerio

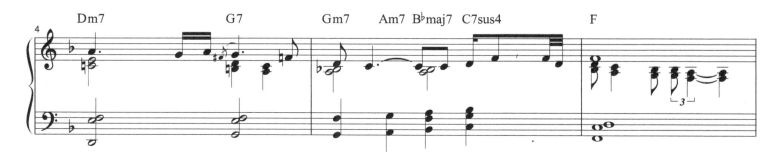

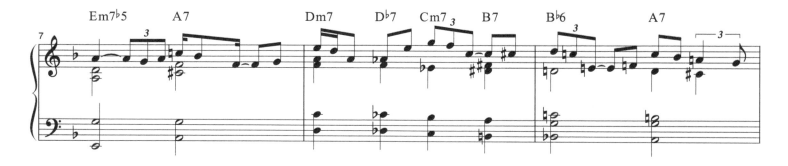

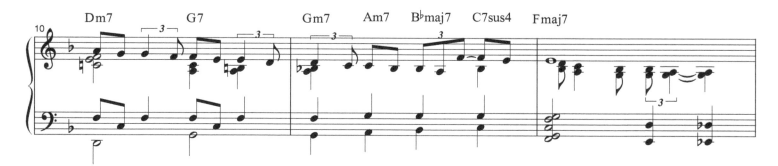

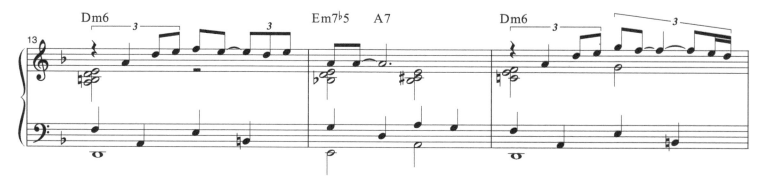

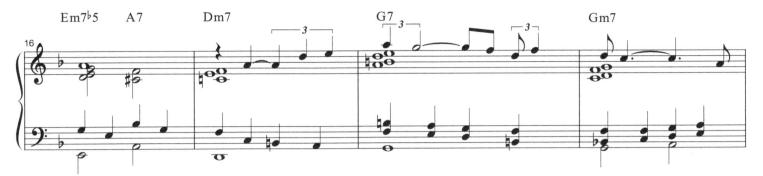

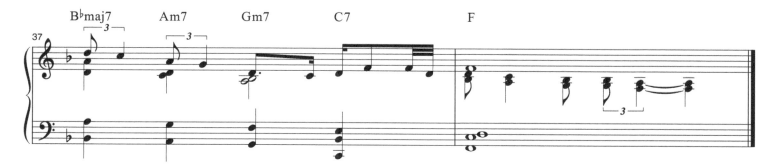

LEAD SHEETS

All five tunes from Chapters 5–9 are written here in lead sheet form. The reader should play these tunes from the lead sheets after studying and playing through the fully written versions in the previous chapters. Characteristic voicings and improvisation techniques of each featured pianist can be used and employed in various ways. The tunes can be interpreted in various ways and the player need not try to imitate the pianists studied in the book.

Playing Along with the Audio Tracks

Tracks 88–92 are full band recordings of the five lead sheet tunes. The piano is isolated on the right stereo channel and the rest of the band is on the left stereo channel. Using *Playback+* online, the reader may listen to the tracks in stereo and then may play along with the band by turning down the right channel. Practice comping during the heads and sax and bass solos, and improvise during the piano solo sections. The reader may turn down the left channel to isolate the piano on the right in order to focus on the piano's comping and improvisations. A road map for each of the band tracks follows.

IN SEARCH OF LOST TIME (BILL EVANS) – TRACK 88

Head (sax)	1 chorus
Sax solo	2 choruses
Piano solo	2 choruses
Bass Solo	2 choruses
Head (sax)	1 chorus
Ending – hold last chord	

DELPHIC DALLIANCE (HERBIE HANCOCK) – TRACK 89

Head (sax)	1 chorus
Sax solo	2 choruses
Piano solo	2 choruses
Head (sax)	1 chorus
Ending – take coda last time	

SOLSTICE (MCCOY TYNER) – TRACK 90

Head (sax)	2 choruses
Sax solo	4 choruses
Piano solo	4 choruses
Head (sax)	2 choruses
Ending – play last four measures two times	

PORTALS (CHICK COREA) – TRACK 91

Head (sax)	1 chorus
Sax solo	3 choruses
Piano solo	3 choruses
Head (sax)	1 chorus
Ending – proceed to last measure	

FORGOTTEN MEMORIES (KEITH JARRETT) – TRACK 92

Head (sax)	1 chorus
Piano solo	1 chorus
Head (sax)	1 chorus
Ending – play measure 27 twenty-eight times	

In Search of Lost Time

John Valerio

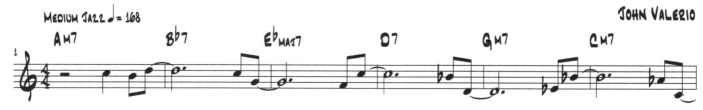

Delphic Dalliance

John Valerio

Medium Jazz ♩ = 154

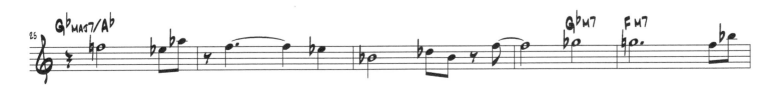

Solstice

Portals

92

Forgotten Memories

John Valerio

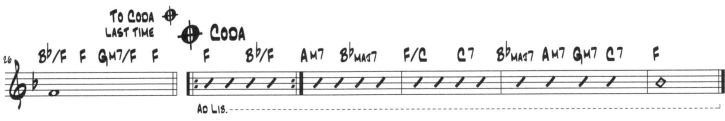

For use with all B-flat, E-flat, Bass Clef and C instruments, the Jazz Play-Along® Series is the ultimate learning tool for all jazz musicians. With musician-friendly lead sheets, melody cues, and other split-track audio choices included, these first-of-a-kind packages help you master improvisation while playing some of the greatest tunes of all time. FOR STUDY, each tune includes a split track with: melody cue with proper style and inflection • professional rhythm tracks • choruses for soloing • removable bass part • removable piano part. FOR PERFORMANCE, each tune also has: an additional full stereo accompaniment track (no melody) • additional choruses for soloing.

1A. MAIDEN VOYAGE/ALL BLUES
00843158 .... $15.99

1. DUKE ELLINGTON
00841644 .... $16.99

2. MILES DAVIS
00841645 .... $16.99

3. THE BLUES
00841646 .... $16.99

4. JAZZ BALLADS
00841691 .... $16.99

5. BEST OF BEBOP
00841689 .... $16.99

6. JAZZ CLASSICS WITH EASY CHANGES
00841690 .... $16.99

7. ESSENTIAL JAZZ STANDARDS
00843000 .... $16.99

8. ANTONIO CARLOS JOBIM AND THE ART OF THE BOSSA NOVA
00843001 .... $16.99

9. DIZZY GILLESPIE
00843002 .... $16.99

10. DISNEY CLASSICS
00843003 .... $16.99

12. ESSENTIAL JAZZ CLASSICS
00843005 .... $16.99

13. JOHN COLTRANE
00843006 .... $16.99

14. IRVING BERLIN
00843007 .... $16.99

15. RODGERS & HAMMERSTEIN
00843008 .... $16.99

16. COLE PORTER
00843009 .... $16.99

17. COUNT BASIE
00843010 .... $16.99

18. HAROLD ARLEN
00843011 .... $16.99

20. CHRISTMAS CAROLS
00843080 .... $16.99

21. RODGERS AND HART CLASSICS
00843014 .... $16.99

22. WAYNE SHORTER
00843015 .... $16.99

23. LATIN JAZZ
00843016 .... $16.99

24. EARLY JAZZ STANDARDS
00843017 .... $16.99

25. CHRISTMAS JAZZ
00843018 .... $16.99

26. CHARLIE PARKER
00843019 .... $16.99

27. GREAT JAZZ STANDARDS
00843020 .... $16.99

28. BIG BAND ERA
00843021 .... $16.99

29. LENNON AND MCCARTNEY
00843022 .... $16.99

30. BLUES' BEST
00843023 .... $16.99

31. JAZZ IN THREE
00843024 .... $16.99

32. BEST OF SWING
00843025 .... $17.99

33. SONNY ROLLINS
00843029 .... $16.99

34. ALL TIME STANDARDS
00843030 .... $16.99

35. BLUESY JAZZ
00843031 .... $16.99

36. HORACE SILVER
00843032 .... $16.99

37. BILL EVANS
00843033 .... $16.99

38. YULETIDE JAZZ
00843034 .... $16.99

39. "ALL THE THINGS YOU ARE" & MORE JEROME KERN SONGS
00843035 .... $16.99

40. BOSSA NOVA
00843036 .... $16.99

41. CLASSIC DUKE ELLINGTON
00843037 .... $16.99

42. GERRY MULLIGAN FAVORITES
00843038 .... $16.99

43. GERRY MULLIGAN CLASSICS
00843039 .... $16.99

45. GEORGE GERSHWIN
00103643 .... $24.99

47. CLASSIC JAZZ BALLADS
00843043 .... $16.99

48. BEBOP CLASSICS
00843044 .... $16.99

49. MILES DAVIS STANDARDS
00843045 .... $16.99

52. STEVIE WONDER
00843048 .... $16.99

53. RHYTHM CHANGES
00843049 .... $16.99

55. BENNY GOLSON
00843052 .... $16.99

56. "GEORGIA ON MY MIND" & OTHER SONGS BY HOAGY CARMICHAEL
00843056 .... $16.99

57. VINCE GUARALDI
00843057 .... $16.99

58. MORE LENNON AND MCCARTNEY
00843059 .... $16.99

59. SOUL JAZZ
00843060 .... $16.99

60. DEXTER GORDON
00843061 .... $16.99

61. MONGO SANTAMARIA
00843062 .... $16.99

62. JAZZ-ROCK FUSION
00843063 .... $16.99

63. CLASSICAL JAZZ
00843064 .... $16.99

64. TV TUNES
00843065 .... $16.99

65. SMOOTH JAZZ
00843066 .... $16.99

66. A CHARLIE BROWN CHRISTMAS
00843067 .... $16.99

67. CHICK COREA
00843068 .... $16.99

68. CHARLES MINGUS
00843069 .... $16.99

71. COLE PORTER CLASSICS
00843073 .... $16.99

72. CLASSIC JAZZ BALLADS
00843074 .... $16.99

73. JAZZ/BLUES
00843075 .... $16.99

74. BEST JAZZ CLASSICS
00843076 .... $16.99

75. PAUL DESMOND
00843077 .... $16.99

78. STEELY DAN
00843070 .... $16.99

79. MILES DAVIS CLASSICS
00843081 .... $16.99

80. JIMI HENDRIX
00843083 .... $16.99

83. ANDREW LLOYD WEBBER
00843104 .... $16.99

84. BOSSA NOVA CLASSICS
00843105 .... $16.99

85. MOTOWN HITS
00843109 .... $16.99

86. BENNY GOODMAN
00843110 .... $16.99

87. DIXIELAND
00843111 .... $16.99

0418

*These do not include split tracks.

KEYBOARD STYLE SERIES

THE COMPLETE GUIDE!

These book/audio packs provide focused lessons that contain valuable how-to insight, essential playing tips, and beneficial information for all players. From comping to soloing, comprehensive treatment is given to each subject. The companion audio features many of the examples in the book performed either solo or with a full band.

BEBOP JAZZ PIANO

by John Valerio

This book provides detailed information for bebop and jazz keyboardists on: chords and voicings, harmony and chord progressions, scales and tonality, common melodic figures and patterns, comping, characteristic tunes, the styles of Bud Powell and Thelonious Monk, and more.

00290535 Book/Online Audio $18.99

BEGINNING ROCK KEYBOARD

by Mark Harrison

This comprehensive book/audio package will teach you the basic skills needed to play beginning rock keyboard. From comping to soloing, you'll learn the theory, the tools, and the techniques used by the pros. The accompanying audio demonstrates most of the music examples in the book.

00311922 Book/Online Audio $14.99

BLUES PIANO

by Mark Harrison

With this book/audio pack, you'll learn the theory, the tools, and even the tricks that the pros use to play the blues. Covers: scales and chords; left-hand patterns; walking bass; endings and turnarounds; right-hand techniques; how to solo with blues scales; crossover licks; and more.

00311007 Book/Online Audio $19.99

BOOGIE-WOOGIE PIANO

by Todd Lowry

From learning the basic chord progressions to inventing your own melodic riffs, you'll learn the theory, tools and techniques used by the genre's best practicioners.

00117067 Book/Online Audio $17.99

BRAZILIAN PIANO

by Robert Willey and Alfredo Cardim

Brazilian Piano teaches elements of some of the most appealing Brazilian musical styles: choro, samba, and bossa nova. It starts with rhythmic training to develop the fundamental groove of Brazilian music.

00311469 Book/Online Audio $19.99

CONTEMPORARY JAZZ PIANO

by Mark Harrison

From comping to soloing, you'll learn the theory, the tools, and the techniques used by the pros. The full band tracks on the audio feature the rhythm section on the left channel and the piano on the right channel, so that you can play along with the band.

00311848 Book/Online Audio $18.99

COUNTRY PIANO

by Mark Harrison

Learn the theory, the tools, and the tricks used by the pros to get that authentic country sound. This book/audio pack covers: scales and chords, walkup and walkdown patterns, comping in traditional and modern country, Nashville "fretted piano" techniques and more.

00311052 Book/Online Audio $19.99

GOSPEL PIANO

by Kurt Cowling

Discover the tools you need to play in a variety of authentic gospel styles, through a study of rhythmic devices, grooves, melodic and harmonic techniques, and formal design. The accompanying audio features over 90 tracks, including piano examples as well as the full gospel band.

00311327 Book/Online Adio $17.99

INTRO TO JAZZ PIANO

by Mark Harrison

From comping to soloing, you'll learn the theory, the tools, and the techniques used by the pros. The accompanying audio demonstrates most of the music examples in the book. The full band tracks feature the rhythm section on the left channel and the piano on the right channel, so that you can play along with the band.

00312088 Book/Online Audio $17.99

JAZZ-BLUES PIANO

by Mark Harrison

This comprehensive book will teach you the basic skills needed to play jazz-blues piano. Topics covered include: scales and chords • harmony and voicings • progressions and comping • melodies and soloing • characteristic stylings.

00311243 Book/Online Audio $17.99

JAZZ-ROCK KEYBOARD

by T. Lavitz

Learn what goes into mixing the power and drive of rock music with the artistic elements of jazz improvisation in this comprehensive book and CD package. This instructional tool delves into scales and modes, and how they can be used with various chord progressions to develop the best in soloing chops.

00290536 Book/CD Pack..$17.95

LATIN JAZZ PIANO

by John Valerio

This book is divided into three sections. The first covers Afro-Cuban (Afro-Caribbean) jazz, the second section deals with Brazilian influenced jazz – Bossa Nova and Samba, and the third contains lead sheets of the tunes and instructions for the play-along audio.

00311345 Book/Online Audio $17.99

MODERN POP KEYBOARD

by Mark Harrison

From chordal comping to arpeggios and ostinatos, from grand piano to synth pads, you'll learn the theory, the tools, and the techniques used by the pros. The online audio demonstrates most of the music examples in the book.

00146596 Book/Online Audio $17.99

NEW AGE PIANO

by Todd Lowry

From melodic development to chord progressions to left-hand accompaniment patterns, you'll learn the theory, the tools and the techniques used by the pros. The accompanying 96-track CD demonstrates most of the music examples in the book.

00117322 Book/CD Pack..$16.99

HAL•LEONARD®

Prices, contents, and availability
subject to change without notice.

www.halleonard.com

POST-BOP JAZZ PIANO

by John Valerio

This book/audio pack will teach you the basic skills needed to play post-bop jazz piano. Learn the theory, the tools, and the tricks used by the pros to play in the style of Bill Evans, Thelonious Monk, Herbie Hancock, McCoy Tyner, Chick Corea and others. Topics covered include: chord voicings, scales and tonality, modality, and more.

00311005 Book/Online Audio $17.99

PROGRESSIVE ROCK KEYBOARD

by Dan Maske

You'll learn how soloing techniques, form, rhythmic and metrical devices, harmony, and counterpoint all come together to make this style of rock the unique and exciting genre it is.

00311307 Book/Online Audio $19.99

R&B KEYBOARD

by Mark Harrison

From soul to funk to disco to pop, you'll learn the theory, the tools, and the tricks used by the pros with this book/audio pack. Topics covered include: scales and chords, harmony and voicings, progressions and comping, rhythmic concepts, characteristic stylings, the development of R&B, and more! Includes seven songs.

00310881 Book/Online Audio $19.99

ROCK KEYBOARD

by Scott Miller

Learn to comp or solo in any of your favorite rock styles. Listen to the audio to hear your parts fit in with the total groove of the band. Includes 99 tracks! Covers: classic rock, pop/rock, blues rock, Southern rock, hard rock, progressive rock, alternative rock and heavy metal.

00310823 Book/Online Audio $17.99

ROCK 'N' ROLL PIANO

by Andy Vinter

Take your place alongside Fats Domino, Jerry Lee Lewis, Little Richard, and other legendary players of the '50s and '60s! This book/audio pack covers: left-hand patterns; basic rock 'n' roll progressions; right-hand techniques; straight eighths vs. swing eighths; glisses, crushed notes, rolls, note clusters and more. Includes six complete tunes.

00310912 Book/Online Audio $18.99

SALSA PIANO

by Hector Martignon

From traditional Cuban music to the more modern Puerto Rican and New York styles, you'll learn the all-important rhythmic patterns of salsa and how to apply them to the piano. The book provides historical, geographical and cultural background info, and the 50+-tracks includes piano examples and a full salsa band percussion section.

00311049 Book/Online Audio $19.99

SMOOTH JAZZ PIANO

by Mark Harrison

Learn the skills you need to play smooth jazz piano – the theory, the tools, and the tricks used by the pros. Topics covered include: scales and chords; harmony and voicings; progressions and comping; rhythmic concepts; melodies and soloing; characteristic stylings; discussions on jazz evolution.

00311095 Book/Online Audio $19.99

STRIDE & SWING PIANO

by John Valerio

Learn the styles of the stride and swing piano masters, such as Scott Joplin, Jimmy Yancey, Pete Johnson, Jelly Roll Morton, James P. Johnson, Fats Waller, Teddy Wilson, and Art Tatum. This book/audio pack covers classic ragtime, early blues and boogie woogie, New Orleans jazz and more. Includes 14 songs.

00310882 Book/Online Audio $19.99

WORSHIP PIANO

by Bob Kauflin

From chord inversions to color tones, from rhythmic patterns to the Nashville Numbering System, you'll learn the tools and techniques needed to play piano or keyboard in a modern worship setting.

00311425 Book/Online Audio $17.99